Water
Precious Water
Book A

EDITORS

Judith Hillen
AIMS Program Director
Fresno Pacific College

Arthur Wiebe
AIMS Program Director
Fresno Pacific College

Dave Youngs
Assistant Program Director
Fresno Pacific College

WRITING TEAM

Maureen Allen
Science Resource Specialist
Irvine Unified School District

Debby Deal
Science Resource Specialist
Irvine Unified School District

Dorothy Terman
Curriculum Coordinator
Irvine Unified School District

Gale Kahn
Science Resource Specialist
Irvine Unified School District

Vincent Sipkovich
Science Resource Specialist
Irvine Unified School District

PRINCIPAL ILLUSTRATORS

Max Cantu
Teacher — Santiago Hills Elementary
Irvine Unified School District

Lori Hammeras
Teacher — Deerfield Elementary
Irvine Unified School District

Contributing Illustrators

Cheryl Johnson, Ellen Small, Chris Kato-Goto, Doug Castleman, Gail Linenbach

Water Precious Water has been developed through a cooperative program involving the AIMS Education Foundation, the California Department of Water Resources, and the Irvine Unified School District.

AIMS (**A**ctivities **I**ntegrating **M**athematics and **S**cience) began in 1981 with a grant from the National Science Foundation. The non-profit AIMS Education Foundation publishes hands-on instructional materials (books and the monthly AIMS Newsletter) that integrate curricular disciplines such as mathematics, science, language arts, and social studies. The Foundation sponsors a national program of professional development through which educators may gain both an understanding of the AIMS philosophy and expertise in teaching by integrated, hands-on methods.

ISBN 1-881431-22-3

Printed in the United States of America

TABLE OF CONTENTS

PROCESS SKILLS AND CONTENT INDEX

	LIFE SCIENCE	EARTH SCIENCE	PHYSICAL SCIENCE
Science Process Skills and Content	*Water Island* (distribution of water resources) *Water Facts* (content) *Were You Aware?* (content)	*Were You Aware?* (content) *Water Facts* (content) *The Water Molecule* (content)	*Water Facts* (content) *Measure Up* (measurement) *Make Your Own Measuring Cup* (calibration) *All Bottled Up* (volume) *How Can We Agree?* (measurement) *Water Olympics* (surface tension, capillary action, density) *Bubble Busters* (surface tension) *Little Bubble Busters* (surface tension)
Water Cycle	*Pond Today Meadow Tomorrow* (succession & evaporation)	*Pond Today Meadow Tomorrow* (succession & evaporation) *Moving Water* (water cycle) *Moving Raindrops* (water cycle) *Mini Water Cycle* (water cycle)	*Moving Water* (water cycle) *Moving Raindrops* (water cycle) *Moving Molecules* (evaporation) *Mini Water Cycle* (water cycle)
Water Quality	*Taste Testers* (survey) *Help Save the Birds* (filtration) *Little Sprouts* (water pollution)	*That Settles It* (succession & evaporation) *Little Sprouts* (water pollution)	*Help Save the Birds* (filtration) *Shake, Foam and Suds* (hard and soft water) *Mini Water Treatment* (simulation)
Water Conservation	*A Little Cup Will Do It* (conservation) *Drip Drop Flip Flop* (water uses) *Water Clock-Shower Timer* (conservation)	*Soil Soakers* (soil absorption) *Rain Away, Don't Rain Away* (erosion/soil absorption)	*Down the Drain* (conservation) *Water Facts* (content) *Moving Molecules* (evaporation)

I HEAR, AND I FORGET

I SEE, AND I REMEMBER

I DO, AND I UNDERSTAND

–Chinese Proverb

Forward

Water is one of our most vital natural resources. It sustains our lives, grows our food, and adds beauty to our world. Yet few of us truly understand or appreciate the wonders of this precious liquid.

To help teachers in K–8 educate their students about "Water Precious Water", this book was developed by AIMS with the cooperation of the California Department of Water Resources and input from water agencies statewide. A special effort was made to design new and exciting classroom activities on water conservation and water quality.

As a scientific and technological government agency, the California Department of Water Resources has a most appropriate role to play in assisting schools. Helping to educate young people in the sciences assures that, in the future, we will have trained personnel to meet the water needs of a continually growing population. We also feel it is important that teachers and students have the educational background to make informed choices on critical water resource issues.

To accomplish these goals, the Department held a series of workshops designed as training sessions on water for teachers. These workshops, done in cooperation with AIMS and members of their leadership network, were cosponsored with local water agencies and school districts. Feedback from teachers at the workshops indicate we developed a highly effective mechanism for providing hands-on classroom activities.

We congratulate AIMS on the activities developed in this book and thank the organization and its highly skilled staff of writers and artists for sharing their ideas.

DWR's Water Education Program offers a broad range of free educational materials on water. Interested teachers may call (916) 322-3070 or (916) 324-2299 or (213) 620-2925 or write Water Education Program, Office of Public Information and Communications, P.O. Box 942836, Sacramento, CA 94236-0001.

Anita Garcia-Fante, Chief
Office of Public Information
and Communications
California Department of Water Resources

Dear Parents,

Our class will be participating in a hands-on math/science unit. The lessons deal with the topic of water. We will do a variety of lessons that combine science processes with mathematical skills.

The water activities will require a variety of materials. We would appreciate your contribution of any of the materials listed below. Please send the materials that you are willing to donate to school by

________________.
date

Thank-you very much,

____
teacher

____
child

Materials List

- styrofoam cups
- plastic cups
- clear plastic cups (3.5 oz)
- baby food jars with lids
- soda containers - 2 liter
- coffee cans - 3 lb size
- plastic containers-(varying sizes)
- 1 box ziplock baggies (qt. size)
- box of salt
- liquid dish soap
- soup cans (10 oz.)
- wax paper
- aluminum foil
- box of straws
- food coloring
- eye droppers
- clean sand
- aquarium charcoal
- box of alum (4 oz.)
- box of toothpicks
- distilled water (1 gal.)
- bottled water (1 gal.)

WERE YOU AWARE?

I. Topic Area
Water awareness

II. Introductory Statement
This activity will have students predict the percentages of salt and fresh water found on the earth and compare their predictions to the actual percentages.

III. Math Skills
a. Estimating
b. Graphing

Science Processes
a. Predicting
b. Recording data
c. Generalizing

IV. Materials
activity sheets
crayons
encyclopedias or other reference books (optional)

V. Key Question
What are the percentages of salt water, fresh water frozen in glaciers and polar ice caps, and fresh surface and ground water available on earth?

VI. Background Information
Water is the second most abundant substance on the face of the earth, but the amount of fresh water available for use is very limited. Most of the water on the earth is salt water which is found in the oceans and seas. Salt water makes up over 97 percent of the water on the earth. Just over two percent of the water on earth is fresh water frozen in glaciers and the polar ice caps. Under one percent of the water on earth is fresh ground water and fresh water in lakes, rivers and streams. About one hundredth of one percent of the water on earth is in the atmosphere. The majority of this fresh water is not easily obtained, making fresh water a very precious resource. Water is continuously changing form but the total amount of water on earth remains constant.

VIII. Procedure
1. Brainstorm as many water sources as possible and categorize them as fresh or salt water.
2. Split the fresh water category into frozen and liquid water categories.
3. Pass out the activity sheets and ask the students to predict the percent of water that would be found in each of three categories; salt water, frozen fresh water in glaciers and the polar ice caps and fresh surface and ground water.
4. Have them color in their predicted percents on the activity sheet.
5. Have students look up the actual percentages in reference books or tell them the correct percentages (97% salt water, 2% frozen fresh water, 1% fresh surface and ground water).
6. Have them complete the activity sheet by coloring in the actual percentages on the activity sheet.

IX. Discussion Questions
1. Discuss the differences between the predicted percentages and the actual percentages for the three categories of water.
2. Discuss the fact that although water is so plentiful on the earth, fresh water is still a valuable resource.
3. Ask the students why they think that the glaciers and polar ice caps are composed of fresh water. They can look up the answer or do the extension activity to find the answer.

X. Extended Activities
1. Have students put a cup of slightly salty water in the freezer.
2. Have them taste both the top and the bottom of the ice and note the differences.
3. Students can look up the local water sources on a map or write to their local water agency to find out where their fresh water comes from.

Were You Aware?

There are 3 different types of water available on Earth: salt water, fresh water in glaciers and polar ice caps, and surface & ground water.

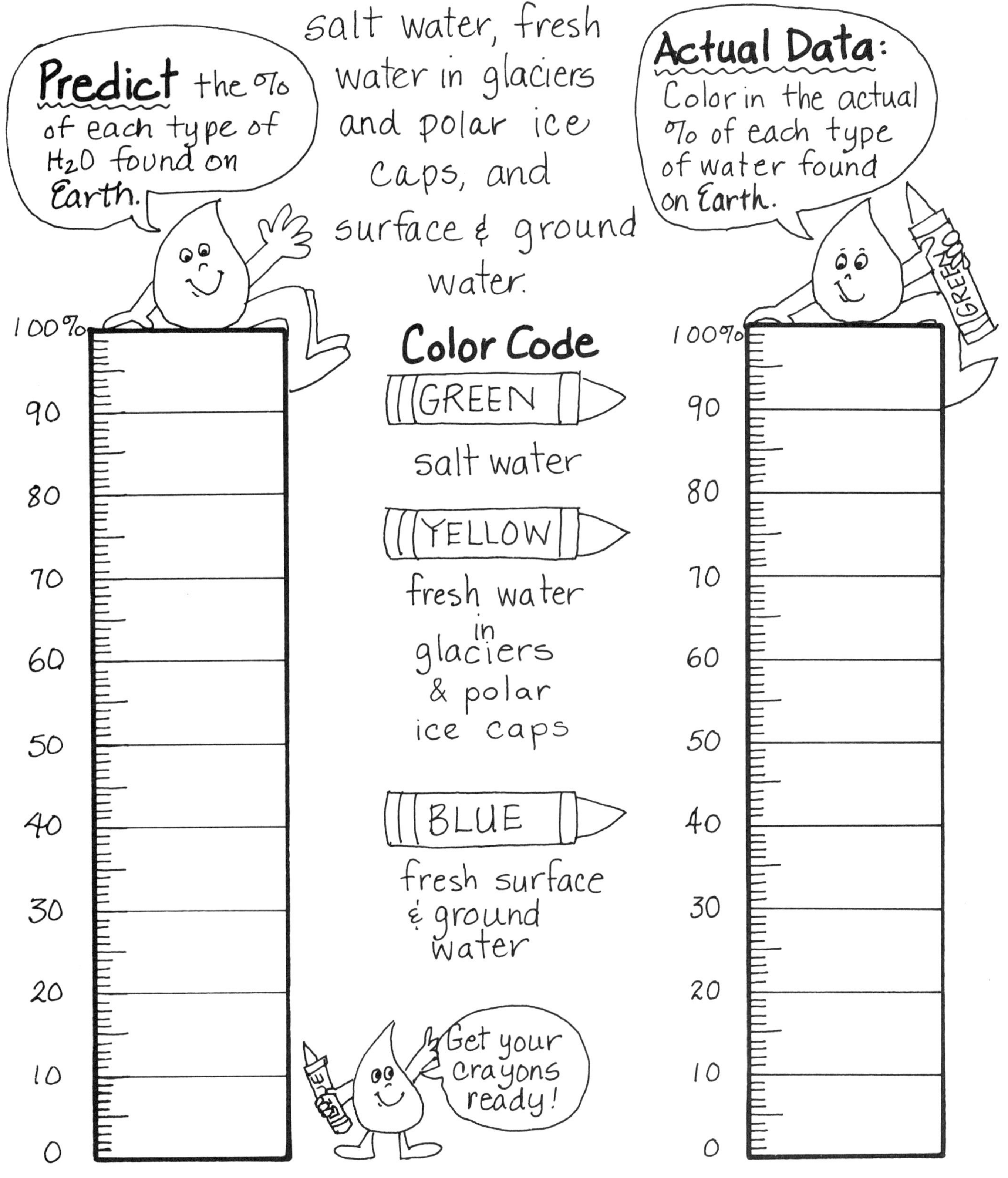

THE WATER MOLECULE

I. Topic Area
Structure of the water molecule

II. Introductory Statement
The students will construct a model of a water molecule. Upper grade students will discuss the distribution of the electrons in the water molecule. Lower grade students may simply cut and glue together the oxygen and hydrogen atoms.

III. Science Processes
a. Collecting and recording data
b. Constructing a model of a water molecule

IV. Materials
1 molecule pattern sheet per student
(Ditto onto construction paper if possible)
water fact sheets
glue
crayons (optional)

V. Key Question
How are electrons in the water molecule arranged?

VI. Background Information
See student water fact sheets.

VIII. Procedure
1. Ask students if they know what water is made of.
2. Pass out the water fact sheets and discuss them with the students.
3. Pass out 1 water moldecule pattern sheet per student. Review the various parts of the water molecule and construct the model in front of the class defining the various parts. Refer to the illustration at the bottom of the fact sheet for the correct placement of the electrons.
4. The upper grade students may cut out and glue the electrons onto the paper atom. Lower grade students may just cut out the 2 hydrogen and oxygen atoms.
5. The students may attach a paper head-band and turn it into a "water molecule hat".

IX. Discussion Questions
1. Review the number and placement of electrons in the atoms in the water molecule.

X. Extended Activities
1. Students may be interested in making other molecule models.
Salt — NaCl
Ammonia — NH_3
Carbon Dioxide — CO_2
Hydrogen Peroxide — H_2O_2

THE WATER MOLECULE
E
HYDROGEN
Oxygen Nucleus
+ 8 Protons
8 Neutrons
Make a water hat!
OXYGEN
HYDROGEN
Hydrogen Nucleus
1 Proton +
1 Proton +
Make a Mobile!

The Water Molecule

All matter is made up of tiny particles called atoms. Atoms are made of even smaller particles called electrons, protons, and neutrons. The protons and neutrons are found in the center of the atom, called the nucleus. The <u>protons</u> have a positive ("+") charge and the <u>neutrons</u> have no charge. The <u>electrons</u> are negatively charged ("–") and spin around the nucleus of the atoms.

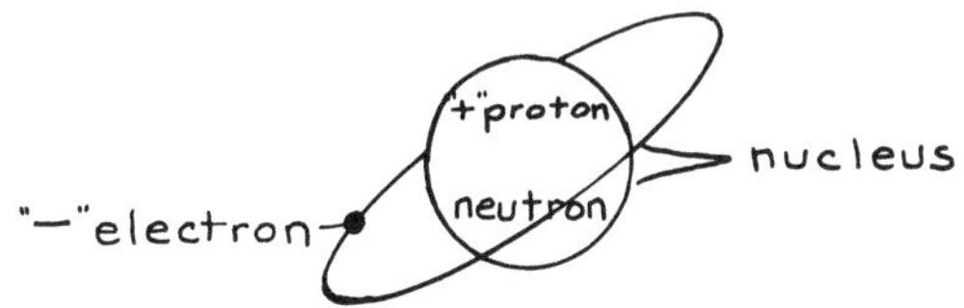

A molecule is a combination of atoms which are bound together. A water molecule combines 2 hydrogen atoms with 1 oxygen atom which are held together by sharing electrons.

$$H_2 + O = H_2O$$

The <u>hydrogen</u> <u>atom</u> has 1 electron spinning around its nucleus. Since the energy level closest to the nucleus may hold up to 2 electrons, hydrogen has room for 1 electron.

1+

room for 1 more electron

The <u>oxygen</u> <u>atom</u> has 8 electrons, 2 in the energy level closest to the nucleus and 6 more in its outer energy level. Since the outer level may hold up to 8 electrons, oxygen has room for 2 more electrons.

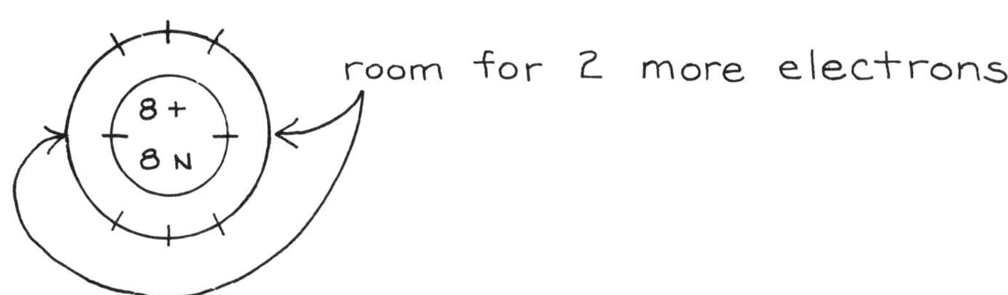

Each of the 2 hydrogen atoms share 1 electron with the 6 electrons from oxygen completing its outer energy level. At the same time, the oxygen atom shares 1 electron with each of the hydrogen atoms completing their outer energy levels.

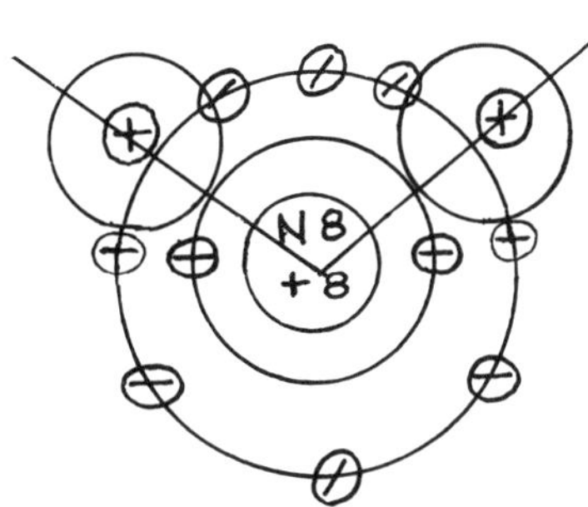

When the water molecule is formed, the electrons from the hydrogen atoms move closer to the oxygen atom making the electron placement unbalanced in the molecule. The hydrogen ends of the molecule then become positively charged ("+") and the oxygen end of molecule negatively charged ("–"). When the ends of a molecule are positively and negatively charged it is said to be a <u>polar molecule.</u> This polar characteristic causes the strong attractive force between water molecules making them a liquid at room temperature.

WATER – A POLAR MOLECULE

<u>Hydrogen</u>
"Positive Charge"

<u>Hydrogen</u>
"Positive Charge"

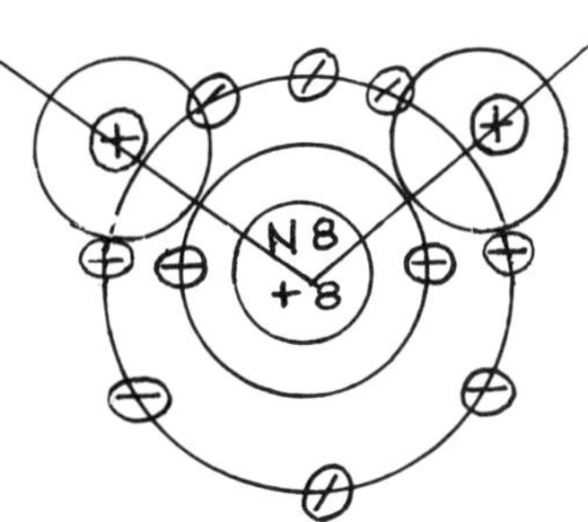

<u>Oxygen</u> – "Negative Charge"

Did you know . . . That 1 drop of water contains 2 million quadrillion molecules = 2,000,000,000,000,000,000,000

MEASURE UP

I. **Topic Area**
Measurement and calibration of a cup

II. **Introductory Statement**
Students will calibrate a cup, observe conservation of volume and use the calibrated cup. The calibrated science cups can be used with many of the lessons that follow.

III. **Math Skills**
a. Predicting
b. Measuring

Science Processes
a. Observation
b. Measuring

IV. **Materials**
Per team:
- 1 beaker that measures 20 ml
- 1 mystery cup (any clear cup)
- masking tape

Individual:
- 1 clear cup (10 ounce Solo, Dixie or other) referred to as science cup
- masking tape strip
- paper clip

Total class:
- 1 bottle dishwashing soap
- 1 bottle corn syrup

V. **Key Question**
How many centimeters high will the 100 milliliter mark be on your science cup?

VI. **Background Information**
To calibrate a cup means to measure and mark the graduations. Conservation of volume is the concept that items hold a given amount.

It's not always true that the tallest or widest container has a greater volume, but whatever the volume, it does not change unless the container shape changes.

Centicubes, the shortest Cuisenaire rods and the unit Dienes blocks are all one cubic centimeter which is equivalent to one milliliter. These objects will help students visualize a milliliter.

VII. **Management Suggestions**
1. Students will work in teams of 3.
2. Students will individually calibrate their science cup and as a team, calibrate the mystery cup.
3. Suggestion: for mystery cups use 6 ounce slant sided Solo cup.
4. Suggestions for bubble maker — bent paper clip or shaped copper wire.

VIII. **Procedure**
1. Students will predict how many centimeters high the 100 ml mark will be on their science cup. Record on activity sheet.
2. Place a piece of masking tape from top to bottom on the outside of the science cup.
3. Taking turns in the team, use the calibrated beaker to measure 20 ml of water and pour into the cup.
4. Mark a line on the tape at water level and record "20 ml".
5. Continue to record each 20 ml measure, until the entire cup has been calibrated. Mark the tape after each 20 ml is added.
6. Using the ruler on the edge of the activity sheet, measure the distance from the bottom of the cup to the 100 ml line. Record on activity sheet.
7. Compute the difference between the prediction and the actual volume of the science cup. Save this cup for future use.
8. Each team is given a "mystery cup". Predict the number of milliliters the cup will hold and how many centimeters from the bottom to the 100 ml mark. Be sure the mystery cup is shaped differently than the science cup.
9. Without teacher input, teams are to calibrate the mystery cup and measure the 100 ml level. Record on chart.
10. Compute the difference between the prediction and the actual volume of the mystery cup.
11. Using the calibrated science cup, teams follow the recipe for bubbles on the activity sheet. Each student should measure at least one item. The bubble mixture should reach the 120 ml line.
12. Students can blow bubbles using paper clips bent in a blower shape.

IX. **Discussion Questions**
1. Is the water level mark of 100 ml the same number of centimeters high on all cups? Why or why not? (conservation of volume)
2. How many uses of the calibrated cup can you think of?

X. **Extended Activities**
1. Use different mystery cups for each team. Find the class cup with the shortest/tallest 100 ml line.
2. Make Jello using the calibrated cups. Note the amount of water used. Now make "finger Jello" which is a reduced water recipe. Note the amount of water to make it. Discuss how water conservation can begin with something as simple as Jello.

XI. **Curriculum Coordinates:**
1. Language: finish these stories — The "Mystery Cup" was filled with. . . or, The magic potion in the "Mystery Cup" turned me into a. . .
2. Art: mix paints (dry tempera and water) using the calibrated cup for measurement.
3. Cooking: follow any recipe using the calibrated cup for measurement.

Measure Up

The Science Cup

	How high is the 100 ml mark?
Prediction	cm
Actual	cm
Difference	cm

The Mystery Cup

	How high is the 100ml mark?	How much did the cup hold?
Prediction	cm	ml
Actual	cm	ml
Difference	cm	ml

The Recipe

20 ml liquid dishwashing soap
20 ml corn syrup
80 ml water

Have fun blowing "bubbles"!

cm measuring tape

0 1 2 3 4 5 6 7 8 9 10 11 12 13 14 15 16 17 18 19 20 21 22 23 24

MAKE YOUR OWN MEASURING CUP

I. Topic Area
Measurement

II. Introductory Statement
Students will calibrate a cup to make their own measuring cup.

III. Math Skills
a. Measurement
b. Whole number operations

Science Processes
a. Measurement
b. Calibration

IV. Materials
1 copy of the activity sheet for each child
scissors
transparent tape
cups that match one of the samples listed

V. Key Question
How can you make your own measuring cup?

VI. Background Information
The tapes found on the activity sheet were calibrated by adding increments of 20 ml of water each time. An 8 ounce cup holds 240 ml. One ounce equals about 30 ml.

VII. Management Suggestions
1. Select cups that match those on the activity sheet.
2. Use transparent tape to cover the entire calibration tape so that it doesn't get wet.

VIII. Procedure
1. Match the top and bottom rims of your cup to the samples on the sheet. Select the correct calibration tape, and tape it to the side of your cup.
2. When finished use a beaker to check the volumes of the cups.
3. Save the measuring cup for use in future lessons that are in this book.

IX. Discussion Questions
1. How many milliliters will fit in the cup?
2. How many cups would it take to make a liter?
3. How could the students use their cup?

X. Extended Activities
1. Use the cup to measure the volume of several containers.
2. Monitor the amount of water that the students drink in a day.

Make Your Own Measuring Cup

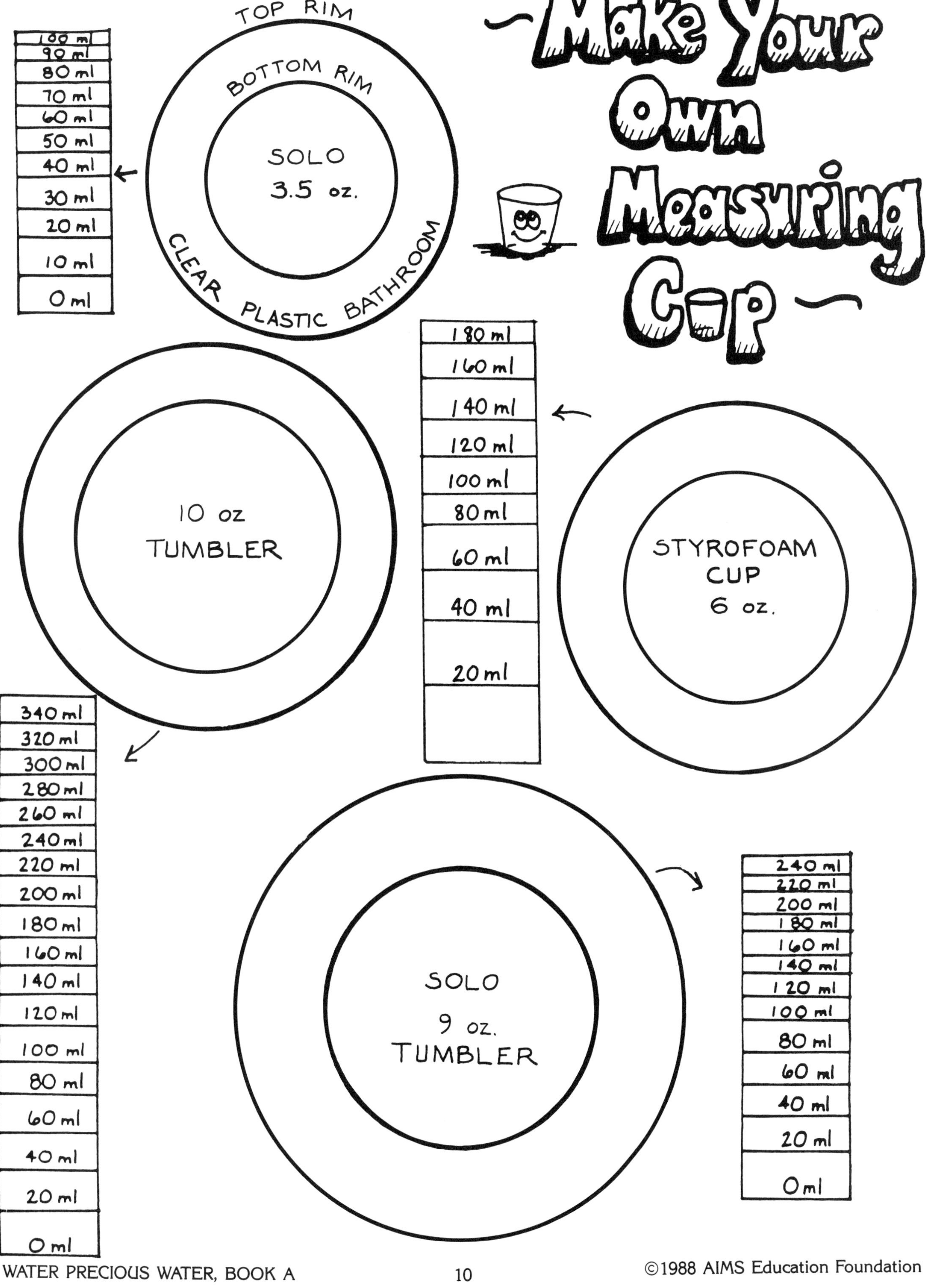

BUBBLE BUSTERS

I. Topic Area
Surface tension of water molecules

II. Introductory Statement
Students will blow bubbles to test the effect of varying amounts of soap on the time a bubble will last.

III. Math Skills
a. Whole number operations
b. Averaging
c. Graphing

Science Processes
a. Observing
b. Predictng
c. Controlling variables
d. Drawing conclusions

IV. Materials
activity sheets
1 box straws
1 pint of dishwashing soap
24 cups (8 ounces)
8 small paper plates or rolls of masking tape
water

V. Key Question
Does the amount of soap in a solution affect the time a bubble will last?

VI. Background Information

Due to the polarity of water molecules, the molecules are attracted to one another. This attraction is called cohesion. Because of cohesion, water molecules below the surface are attracted equally in all directions. The molecules on the surface, however, are only attracted to the sides and down. This makes water act as if it has a "skin" on its surface. This phenomenon is called surface tension. The surface tension of water is strong enough so that the water molecules will not stretch enough to form lasting bubbles. When water becomes soapy, the attractive forces on its surface become weaker. This allows bubbles to be formed by blowing air into the soapy mixture. The pull of tension in the soap film shapes the soapy water into a bubble, but does not allow the bubbles to burst as fast as plain water bubbles. Soap molecules and water molecules attract one another (this attraction of unlike molecules is called adhesion) and distribute themselves in layers. Two layers of soap molecules sandwich a layer of water molecules. This arrangement stretches more easily than a single layer of water and also pulls apart more slowly.

Bubbles will appear black just before they burst. When ordinary light strikes the soap bubble, light is reflected from the front and back surfaces of the film. Due to irregular interference bright colors appear. The colors change as the thickness of the film changes during evaporation. As the thickness of the film becomes smaller than the wave length of ordinary light, there is destructive interference of all light and the bubble appears black.

VII. Management Suggestions
1. Fill four one liter containers with water and label A, B, C, and D. Put ½ teaspoon of liquid dish soap in A, 5 teaspoons in B, 15 teaspoons in C and 30 teaspoons in D. Dawn dish soap works well.
2. The students can use the top of their desk to blow the bubbles on or use a desk cover such as aluminum foil or plastic. Using the desk top provides an excellent opportunity for the students to clean their desk. (Rinse desks with a vinegar and water solution to cut soap film.)
3. Have students work in groups of 4. Each student will get to blow 3 bubbles of the 12 on the data table.
4. Students should time the bubbles in seconds, i.e., 1 minute 20 seconds = 80 seconds.
5. Wet the table top with water or soap solution so that the bubbles will adhere to the water molecules on the table. A dry table will cause the bubble to burst immediately.

VIII. Procedure
1. Pass out to each group the following — 4 straws, 1 small paper plate, 4 bubble solutions (cup A, cup B, cup C, cup D), paper towels, and the activity sheets.
2. Demonstrate blowing a bubble by putting a straw into soapy water. Remove some solution by putting your finger over the top of the straw and placing the soapy end of the straw on a slightly wet table. Place the straw at a 45° angle. Blow gently into the pool of soapy water that is around the end of the straw. Blow a bubble that is approximately 6″ in diameter. Time how long it takes for the bubble to burst.
3. Discuss the importance of having the bubbles the same size. Explain that the students will trace a small paper plate on the table. Use a pencil to trace this circle so that it can be easily erased. The students will blow the bubbles to the size of the circle drawn on the table.
4. Explain that each group will blow 12 bubbles (3 for each solution A, B, C, and D). Have the students decide on a plan to equitably involve all group members in the timing and blowing of the bubbles. Be sure the table top is wet to begin with.
5. Discuss the question on the activity sheet and make predictions.
6. Gather the data and complete the chart. Graph the data. Students will have to decide on the increments on the graph. They should look at the range of the data and decide on whether to number the seconds by 5, 10, 20, or 25 second increments.
7. Draw conclusions and discuss other variables that may have affected the data i.e. — each successive bubble benefited from the soap that was on the desk from the previous bubble.

IX. Discussion Questions
1. What is surface tension?
2. How did the amount of soap affect the time the bubbles lasted?
3. Does adding more soap always produce longer lasting bubbles? Why?
4. Examine the bubbles carefully. What happens to the color of the bubbles just before they burst?

X. Extended Activities
1. Try using various kinds of soap to see how long a bubble will last.
2. Find the cost of making your own bubble solution and compare it to the cost of commercially sold solutions.
3. See who can blow the largest bubble. Try adding glycerin or Karo Syrup to the bubble mixture.
4. See lesson 1, "Measure Up" for a bubble recipe.

Name ______________

Question: Does the amount of soap in a solution affect the time a bubble will last?

Predictions: Which solution will make bubbles that last the longest?

Rank the solutions in order from the longest to the shortest lasting bubbles.

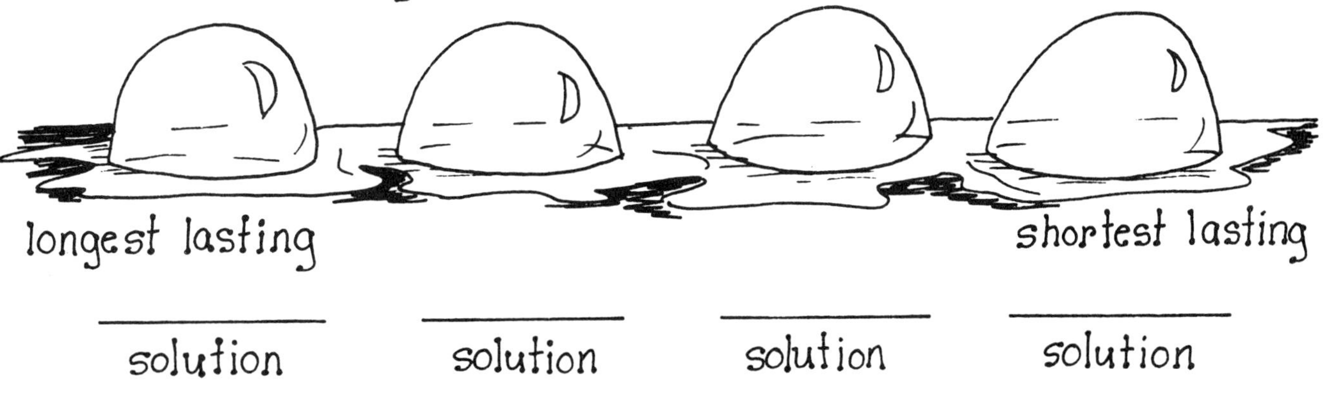

longest lasting — shortest lasting

______ solution ______ solution ______ solution ______ solution

Why did you rank them as you did? ______________________________

____

____

Data Gathering:

solution	Trial 1 (Time in Seconds)	Trial 2	Trial 3	Totals	÷ # of trials	Average Time
A		+	+	=	÷ 3	=
B		+	+	=	÷ 3	=
C		+	+	=	÷ 3	=
D		+	+	=	÷ 3	=

Average Time Bubbles Lasted in Seconds

A B C D

Solutions

Conclusions:

1) Which bubble had the longest average time?____ Why do you think it did?______

______

______

2) Which bubble had the shortest average time?____ Why do you think it did?______

______

______

3) What other variables could have affected this experiment?___

______

______

LITTLE BUBBLE BUSTERS

I. Topic Area
Bubbles.

II. Introductory Statement
Students will blow bubbles using different solutions, determining the solution that makes the longest lasting bubbles.

III. Math Skills
a. Measuring
b. Comparing
c. Graphing

Science Processes
a. Predicting
b. Gathering data
c. Applying and generalizing

IV. Materials
cups
Dawn or other liquid soap
food coloring
watch or clock with second hand
paper plates
straws
activity sheets

V. Key Question
Which bubble solution will produce the longest lasting bubbles?

VI. Background Information
See background section of "Bubble Busters", which is included in this book.

VII. Management Suggestions
1. Prepare the solutions as follows:
   Yellow: ½ t. soap, 1 liter water, 1 drop yellow
   Green: 5 t. soap, 1 liter water, 1 drop green
   Red: 15 t. soap, 1 liter water, 1 drop red
   Blue: 30 t. soap, 1 liter water, 1 drop blue
   Note: The spoons drawn above the cups on the activity sheet do not show the actual amount of soap in each cup, they only show that solution A has the least soap, D the most.
2. Set up a butcher paper graph with the following time intervals marked: less than 30 seconds; 30-60 seconds; over 60 seconds.
   Note: You may need to modify these time intervals. The amount of humidity will affect the length of time a bubble will last since evaporation plays an important part in the popping of a bubble.

VIII. Procedure
1. Discuss key question. Have students support their predictions.
2. Review procedures and materials:
   a. Put students in groups of four. Assign a different solution (blue, green, red or yellow) to each member of the group.
   b. Pass out a paper plate to each student. Discuss why the bubbles in this experiment need to be a standard size.
   c. Students coat the plate with a thin soap solution using their fingers.
   d. Using a straw, students blow a bubble on the flat part of their plate. See "Bubble Busters" for bubble blowing instructions.
   e. Allow time for students to practice blowing the bubbles.
3. Actual Test
   a. Explain the activity sheet: remind students that the group timer or teacher will call out at the end of 30 and 60 seconds.
   b. Emphasize that all students must begin at the same time.
   c. Record predictions on the activity sheets.
   d. Perform the experiment.
   e. Record results on the activity sheet.
   f. Students color the graph tag the same color as their solution, sign it, and cut it out.
4. Make a class graph using each student's graph tag. Place the colored tags in the proper column on the butcher paper graph.
5. Determine solution that produces the longest lasting bubbles.
6. Compare predictions with the results.

IX. Discussion Questions
1. Which color solution made the most bubbles that lasted over 60 seconds?
2. Why didn't all bubbles from that solution last the same time?
3. Which color solution produced the shortest lasting bubbles?
4. What can you say about the amount of soap that goes into the "perfect" solution?
5. What time interval on the graph has the most tags? What does that mean?

X. Extended Activities
1. Students can experiment with soap and water combinations to find the "perfect" bubble solution.
2. Have students make a variety of bubble blowing devices.

XI. Curriculum Coordinates:
1. Creative Writing: Write a story about the "Adventures of My Bubble".
2. Art: Rainbow-Squares — fold paper towel into fourths. Dip each corner of folded towel into a different solution. The colors will spread into one another. Allow to dry.

LITTLE BUBBLE BUSTERS

What do I want to find out?:

Which bubble solution will make bubbles that last the longest; A, B, C, D?

Circle the bubble solution you think will make the longest lasting bubbles.

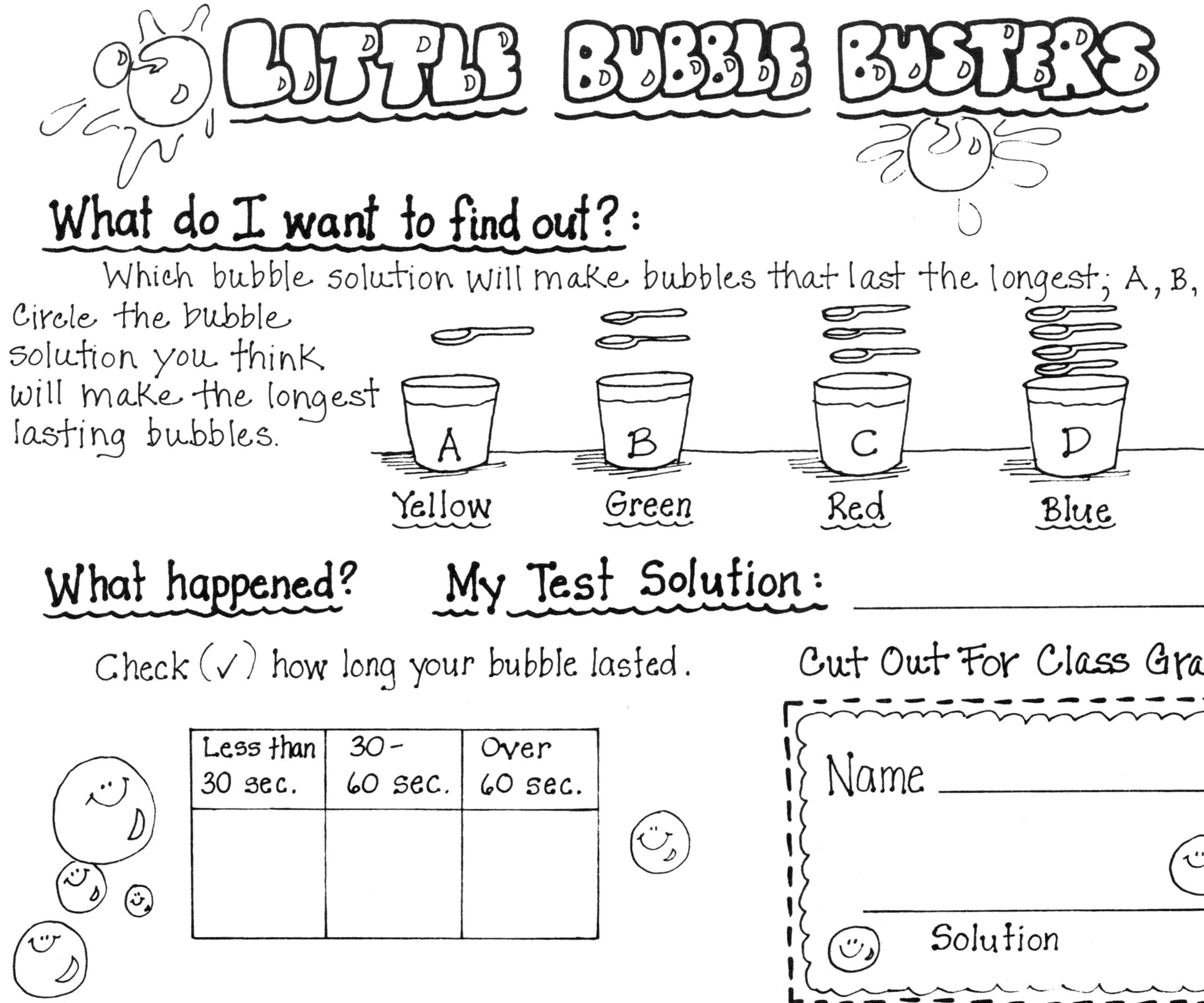

What happened?

My Test Solution: ____________________

Check (✓) how long your bubble lasted.

Less than 30 sec.	30 - 60 sec.	Over 60 sec.

Cut Out For Class Graph

Name ____________________

____
Solution

ALL BOTTLED UP

I. Topic Area
Conservation of volume

II. Introductory Statement
Students will compare the capacities of 4 different bottles, predicting and observing the various volumes of water each can hold.

III. Math Skills
a. Predicting
b. Graphing
c. Measuring
d. Sequencing

Science Processes
a. Comparing
b. Collecting and recording data
c. Measuring
d. Observing
e. Classifying
f. Estimating

IV. Materials
Per team:
4 bottles — each a different shape (ideas: individual seltzer, soda, shampoo, syrup, canning jar)
water pitcher
measuring cup beaker or graduated cylinder
paper towels

V. Key Question
Which bottle do you think holds the most water?

VI. Background Information
The capacity of a bottle is the amount that it holds. This is measured in milliliters. With irregularly shaped containers, it is difficult to predict the volume of liquid it will hold. *Note:* It is not always true that the tallest or widest bottle holds the greatest volume.

VII. Management Suggestions
1. Be sure students have brought in or you have collected a variety of bottles. Group the bottles in sets of four so that they are somewhat similar in size but do not hold the same amount of water. Label the sets of bottles A, B, C, D with tape or stickers.
2. Students should be in teams of 4–6.
3. Allow 40–50 minutes for this activity.

VIII. Procedure
1. Introduction
   a. Team will sketch the 4 bottles in the squares on the top of the activity sheet.
   b. Students predict which bottle will hold the most. . . least.
   c. Students will list their predictions in order of most to least on the activity sheet.
2. Activity
   a. Fill the first bottle with water from the pitcher.
   b. Pour it from the bottle into measuring cup — record amount on data table.
   Note: You can present your students with a problem solving activity by including bottles which hold more than the graduated cylinders.
3. The data
   a. Students fill in "actual" by listing bottles in order: from holding the most to holding the least.
   b. Using data collected, students prepare the graph.

IX. Discussion Questions
1. Were the predictions correct?
2. If not, what do you notice about the bottle that holds the most water.
3. Let's find the SUPER BOTTLE, the class bottle that holds the most water.
   a. Teams bring their bottles that held the most to the front of the class.
   b. These bottles are re-labelled a,b,c,d,e. . .
   c. Students list their predictions in order most to least on SUPER BOTTLE activity sheet.
   d. Now teams share with class the data on their bottle. Students record the number of milliliters on the data table.
   e. Students compare data and list the bottles in order from the bottle that holds the most to the one that holds the least.
4. Were your predictions correct?
5. What shape does this SUPER BOTTLE have?
6. Is it always true that the tallest bottle holds the most?
7. Is it always true that the widest bottle holds the most?

X. Extended Activities
1. Try the activity again with a different liquid or sand. Do you get the same results? Does the volume held differ with different types of "fillers".
2. Try the activity with different types of containers such as boxes, cans, etc.

XI. Curriculum Coordinates
1. Language Arts: Suggested titles to be used in the "All Bottled Up" creative writing blank.
   a. What would you want your mom to put into a SUPER BOTTLE and why?
   b. The bottle has floated in from somewhere — there's a message inside, what does it say?
   c. Tell a story about where the bottle has been.
   d. The genie suddenly popped out of the bottle granting three wishes. What wishes would you want? Why?
2. Art:
   a. Decorate your bottle.
   b. Design a bottle. Tell why you designed it that particular shape and what its use will be.
3. Music: Using the bottles from the lesson, create a musical instrument and as a team, play a song for the class.
4. Social Studies:
   a. If you were to recycle the bottle, what else could it be used for?
   b. Research how glass bottles are produced.

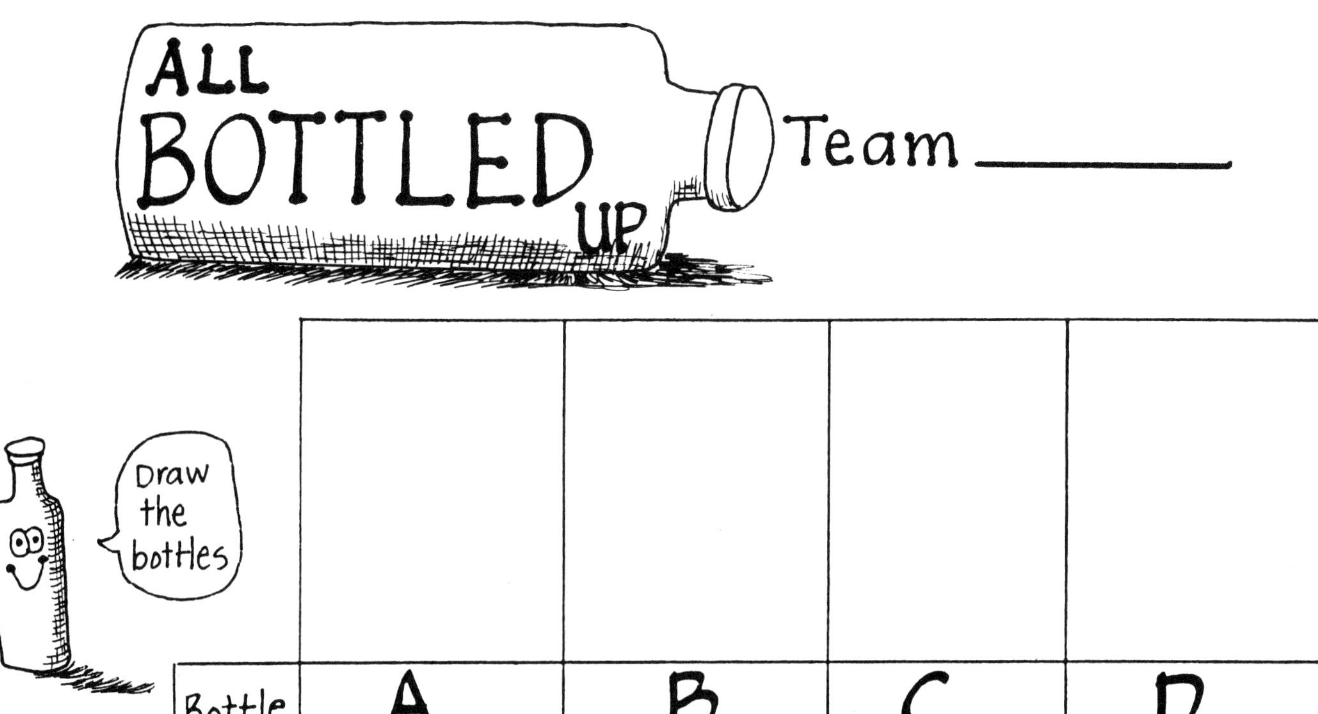
ALL BOTTLED UP
Team ________
Draw the bottles
Bottle
A
B
C
D

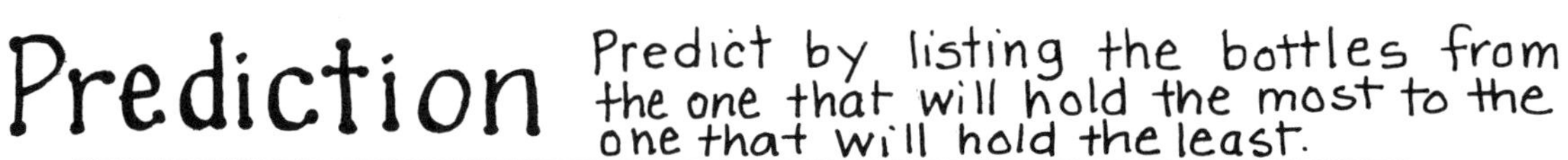
Prediction
Predict by listing the bottles from the one that will hold the most to the one that will hold the least.

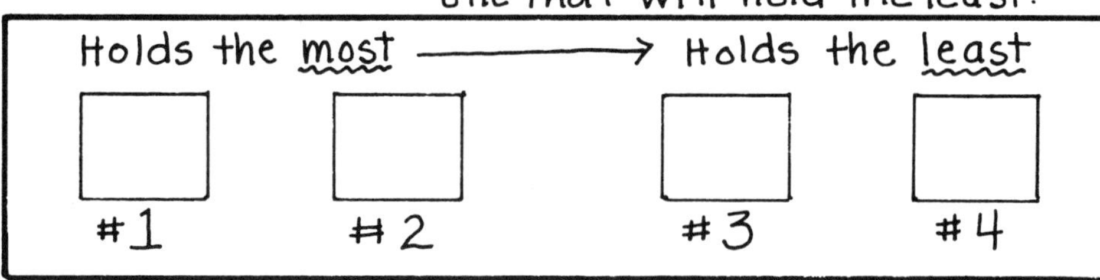
Holds the most → Holds the least
#1
#2
#3
#4

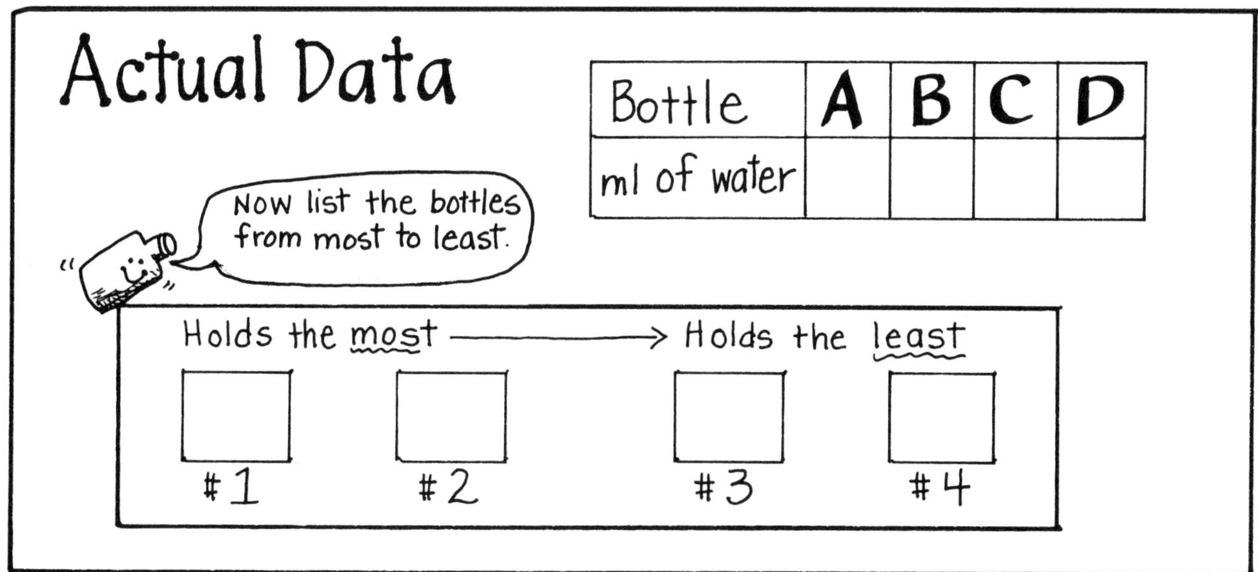
Actual Data
Bottle
A
B
C
D
ml of water
Now list the bottles from most to least.
Holds the most → Holds the least
#1
#2
#3
#4

Team ____________

ALL BOTTLED UP

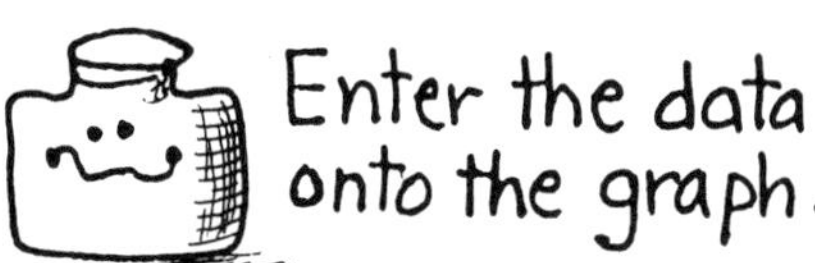

Enter the data onto the graph.

Find the bottle that holds the most water and the bottle that holds the least.

DATA TABLE				
400 ml				
380 ml				
360 ml				
340 ml				
320 ml				
300 ml				
280 ml				
260 ml				
240 ml				
220 ml				
200 ml				
180 ml				
160 ml				
140 ml				
120 ml				
100 ml				
80 ml				
60 ml				
40 ml				
20 ml				
	Bottle A	Bottle B	Bottle C	Bottle D
DATA	___ ml	___ ml	___ ml	___ ml

SUPER BOTTLE

PREDICTION

Predict by listing the bottles from the one that will hold the most to the one that will hold the least.

MOST ——————————————> **LEAST**

#1	#2	#3	#4	#5	#6	#7	#8

DATA

Bottle	a	b	c	d	e	f	g	h
ml. of water								

ACTUAL

#2	#3	#4	#5	#6	#7	#8

ALL BOTTLED UP
Name

HOW CAN WE AGREE?

I. Topic Area

Estimating and measuring volume

II. Introductory Statement

Students will estimate and measure the amount of water a can holds and come up with a group concensus as to its volume.

III. Math Skills

a. Estimating volume
b. Measuring volume
c. Whole number calculation

Science Processes

a. Predicting
b. Recording data
c. Controlling variables

IV. Materials

8 identical tin cans (soup can size)
8 graduated cylinders or measuring cups
Paper towels

V. Key Question

Can your group agree on the volume of a can?

VI. Background Information

All measurements are approximate and vary in degrees of accuracy. Precise measurements are difficult to make and take great attention to detail and precision equipment. Students will measure the volume of a can and may get different answers. Scientists also may get varying results in doing the same experiment and seek to validate each other's work. The students will work together to come to an agreement on the volume of a can. Repeated trials and collaboration may be necessary to reach a consensus. Controlling variables can help make the results more accurate.

VII. Management Suggestions

1. Use soup cans or other similar sized tin cans with the labels removed. Make sure they are all the same size.
2. Make sure the volume is not printed on the can.
3. Use graduated cylinders marked in small increments, if available.

VIII. Procedure

1. Divide the students into groups of 3 or 4 and make sure each group has a can, a graduated cylinder and some water.
2. Have the students estimate the volume of their group's can and record it on the activity sheet.
3. Each group will then measure the volume of their can and come to a consensus on the answer and record it on the activity sheet.
4. Have each group report its results to the class and have everyone record those results on the activity sheet for trial 1.
5. After discussing the importance of measuring things more than once, have the groups estimate and measure the volume again. Share the results and fill in the blanks on the activity sheet for trial 2.
6. Discuss the results. Even though the cans are identical, measurement errors and other variables will generally cause a wide range of answers. Discuss, as a class, ways to control variables and get more accurate results. Emphasize the fact that even the most accurate measurements are not exact (this may be a good time to introduce the concept of tolerances).
7. Put the 8 smaller groups together in pairs to get 4 larger groups (if possible, put together groups that got different answers). Have the 4 large groups repeat the same activities that the 8 smaller groups just completed and record the answers on the activity sheet.
8. Discuss the results. Do the groups all get the same answers? Why or why not? If the answers for the 4 groups are not the same can the class agree on an answer? How?

XI. Discussion

1. Why were the answers different?
2. Why was it difficult to agree on an answer?
3. Is it always important to be precise in measuring? Give examples to defend your answers.

X. Extensions

1. Repeat the same kind of activity with some other form of measurement, for example, have each group cut a piece of string 12 meters long and compare them.
2. Write a story about a person who always measures incorrectly and the problems it causes.

Name ____________

How Can We Agree?

How much do I hold?

Question: How many ml of water does our can hold?

Step 1

Prediction:	Trial 1	ml	Actual Trial 1	ml
Prediction:	Trial 2	ml	Actual Trial 2	ml

Step 2

Class Data: Record the data for each group.

Group	Volume Trial 1	Volume Trial 2
1		
2		
3		
4		
5		
6		
7		
8		

Do all the groups agree on the actual volume? ☐ yes ☐ no

If not, why? ____________

Who is correct?

Step 3

Combined groups #'s	Volume Trial 1	Volume Trial 2

Do all the groups agree on the actual volume? ☐ yes ☐ no

If not, why? ____________

Step 4

How can we agree on an answer? ____________

Final= ml

THE MINI WATER CYCLE

I. Topic Area
Water cycle

II. Introductory Statement
This activity will demonstrate the processes of evaporation and condensation within a miniature water cycle inside a plastic bag.

III. Math Skills	**Science Processes**
a. Measuring	a. Observing
	b. Recording
	c. Generalizing

IV. Materials
quart size zip-lock baggies
bathroom size, clear plastic Solo cups — 3.5 oz.
masking tape

V. Key Question
What happens to liquid water when it evaporates in a closed system such as a zip-locked baggie?

VI. Background Information
See background information on water cycle information. As the water *evaporates,* it is invisible. As the water vapor cools (or slows down its molecular motion) it *condenses* and returns to a liquid state. Water droplets may form at the top and sides and slowly collect at the bottom of the baggie.

VII. Management Suggestions
1. Be sure to tape the baggie on an angle, like a diamond, so that the sides will slant down from the top allowing the droplets to slide down and collect in the bottom of the baggie.
2. Place in a sunny, warm spot.
3. You may need to tape the cup to the inside of the baggie so that the water will not tip over.

VIII. Procedure
1. Review with the students the natural water cycle stressing the processes of evaporation, condensation, precipitation, and accumulation.
2. Tell students they will create a very simple water cycle in a closed baggie and observe how water invisibly *evaporates* from the cup, like it does from oceans, *condenses* on the sides of the baggie, like it does in the clouds and accumulates in the bottom of the baggie like it does in lakes, rivers and ground water.
3. Pass out a baggie and cup to each student, or group of students. Place approximately 2 ounces of water in the cup and mark the water line. Tape the cup to the inside of baggie to prevent spilling.
4. Close the baggie tightly and tape it in a warm place, tilted on an angle like a diamond. See activity sheet.
5. Pass out student observation sheet and record what happens over a 4 day period.

What the Students will do:
1. Assemble the mini-solar still.
2. Observe the changes over a 4-day period.
3. Draw pictures of the changes.

IX. Discussion Questions
1. Correlate the various steps of the natural water cycle to the cycle in the baggie. See "Moving Water" lesson in this book.
2. Ask students what they think will happen to the water in the cup.
3. How does the place where the mini water cycle is put affect the amount of water that collects in the bottom of the baggie?
4. What would happen if the solar still was left in a warm place for 1 month?

X. Extended Activities
1. Perform the same experiment again with salt water instead of plain water. This is one method of desalination, that is, separating salt from salt water by evaporation.
2. Perform the same experiment varying the light, color of baggie, amount of water, size of baggie, etc.
3. Perform the same experiment using different liquids such as, milk, rubbing alcohol, 7-Up.
4. Add food coloring to the water to represent contaminates. Observe whether or not the food coloring can evaporate.

XI. Curriculum Coordinates
1. Language Arts: Write a story of how someone could survive with minimal water using the "water cycle in a baggie" concept.
2. Critical thinking: Design a self-watering plant container based on the "mini water cycle".
3. Math: Measure the number of milliliters of water that was evaporated from the cup over a 4-day period.

The Mini Water Cycle

✱ Place your mini water cycle in a warm or sunny place.

DRAW A PICTURE OF WHAT HAPPENED TO THE WATER IN THE CUP.

1 Draw a picture at the beginning of the experiment.

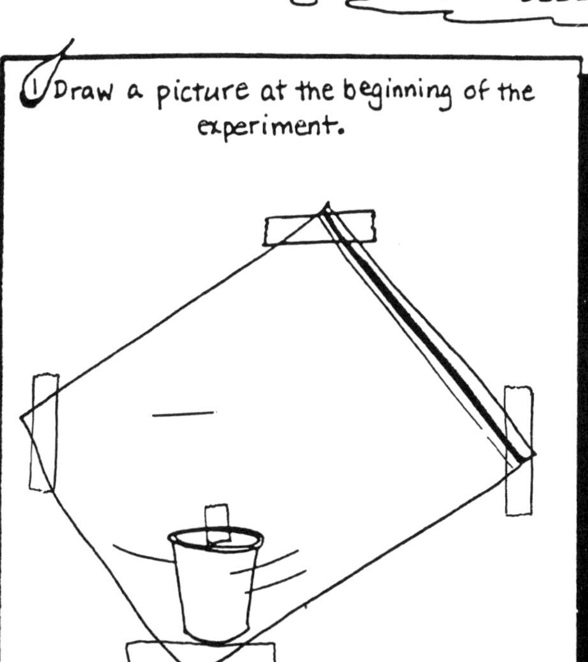

2 Draw picture after **two** hours.

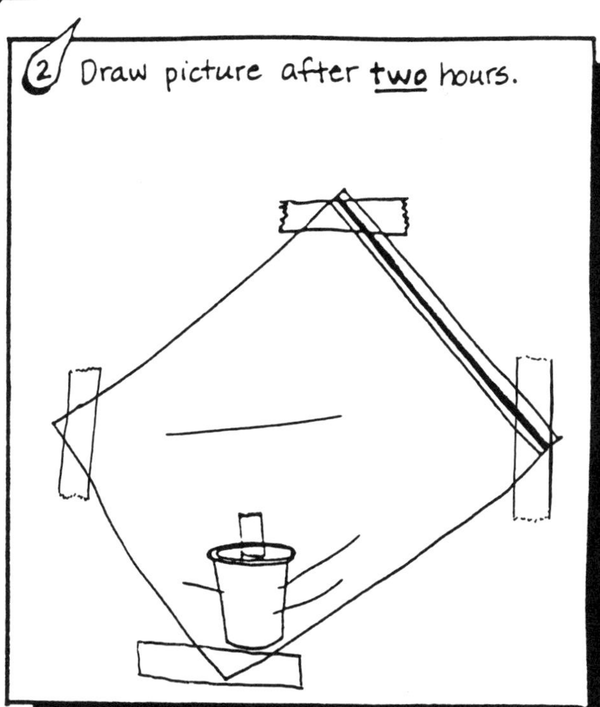

3 Draw a picture on **Day 2**.

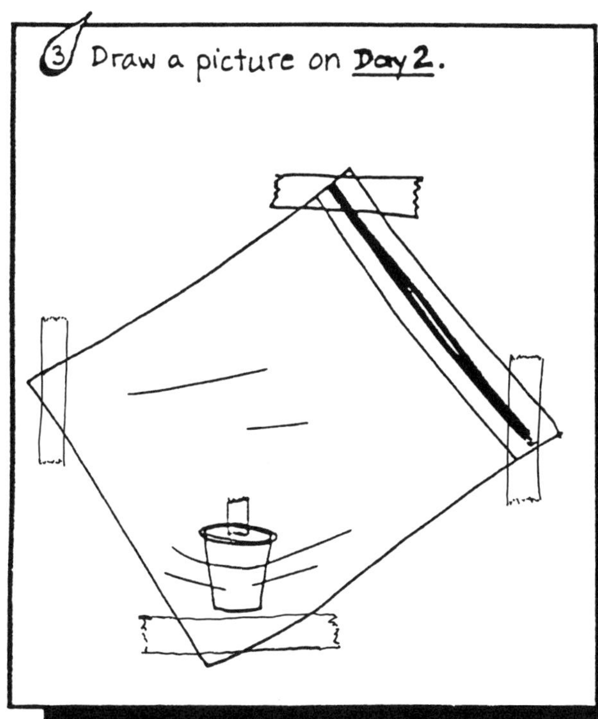

4 Draw a picture on **Day 4**

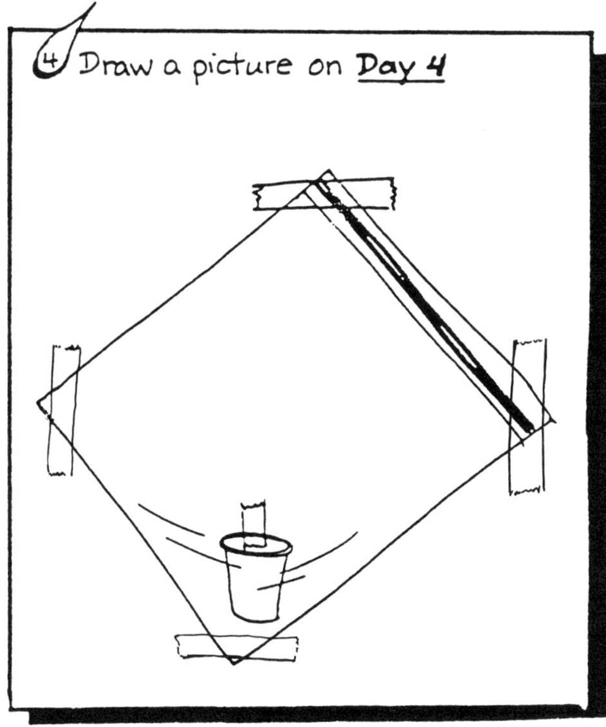

MOVING WATER

I. Topic Area

Water cycle: evaporation and condensation

II. Introductory Statement

This lesson will use a demonstration to introduce the concept of water changing forms through the process of *evaporation* and *condensation.*

III. Science Processes

a. Observing
b. Generalizing

IV. Materials

For class demonstration:
- 1 hot plate
- 1 teakettle
- 2 large metal (aluminum) baking pans
- 1 tray ice cubes

Per student:
- activity sheet
- scissors and crayons

V. Key Question

What different forms will water take when it is heated or cooled?

VI. Background Information

This demonstration will bridge the gap between the concrete, real-life experience of boiling water in the kitchen to the more abstract concept of the "water cycle".

The "water cycle" can briefly be described as the continuous movement of the earth's water from the oceans, to the air and back to the ocean and land again.

The heat from the sun *evaporates* the water from the land and the ocean. The cool air *condenses* the water vapor into water droplets or ice crystals. They fall to the ground and the oceans in a process called *precipitation.*

In this demonstration, the water is heated by the hot plate instead of the sun. The water vapor is invisible and may be found in the neck of the teakettle and just above the spout. The steam represents the *condensed* water vapor in the air as it cools. It is more visible as a liquid when it collects on the bottom of the metal baking pan as water droplets. As the droplets fall to the ground, you can compare that to precipitation or "rain".

Around 75% of the precipitation falls back directly on the oceans. The rest evaporates immediately from the ground or different surfaces or may soak into the earth and become part of the ground water supply. Eventually, much of the surface and ground water returns to the oceans, beginning the entire process over again. Thus the name "water cycle".

VII. Management Suggestions

1. Gather a teakettle, hotplate, 2 large aluminum baking pans and a tray of ice cubes for the water cycle demonstration.
2. Run off a "Moving Water" activity sheet for each student.

VIII. Procedure

1. Have students observe a steaming teakettle and describe what they see happening.
2. Ask: "What is the steam made of?" "Where did it come from?"
3. Ask: "Is there some way we can get the steam or water vapor to return to a liquid state?" hint. . . "How did they get the liquid to go to vapor?" "How can we get it to go from a vapor to a liquid?" "Can you think of something we use to cool down a substance quickly?"
4. Fill a large aluminum pan with ice and place over steaming teakettle. Observe and discuss.
5. When enough water droplets appear — shake pan downward slightly and ask "What form of water does this remind you of?"
6. Ask: "Can you figure out a way to collect the water drops and return them to the teakettle?"
7. Discuss how scientists have assigned names to the different changes water undergoes in the demonstration they have just seen. Discuss and define each.
   a. From liquid to vapor — Evaporation
   b. From vapor back to liquid — Condensation
8. Stress that the water is undergoing a change in form but the water molecule always remains the same. The energy level of the water molecule affects whether it is a solid, liquid, or gas.

What the Students Will Do:

1. Pass out copies of the activity sheet (or have students draw their own — labeling the changes water undergoes during the demonstration, mainly — evaporation and condensation).
2. Students should cut out "drops" and "water vapor" strips.
3. Cut slits on dotted lines and insert paper strips.
4. Students should explain the changes the liquid water undergoes in the demonstration on the lines below the picture.
5. Cut out the cloud and the mountain lake scene. Ask students what objects in the demonstration picture perform the same function in nature. Cut out the clouds and fit them over the pan of ice cubes and put the mountain lake scene over the cookie sheet and teakettle.

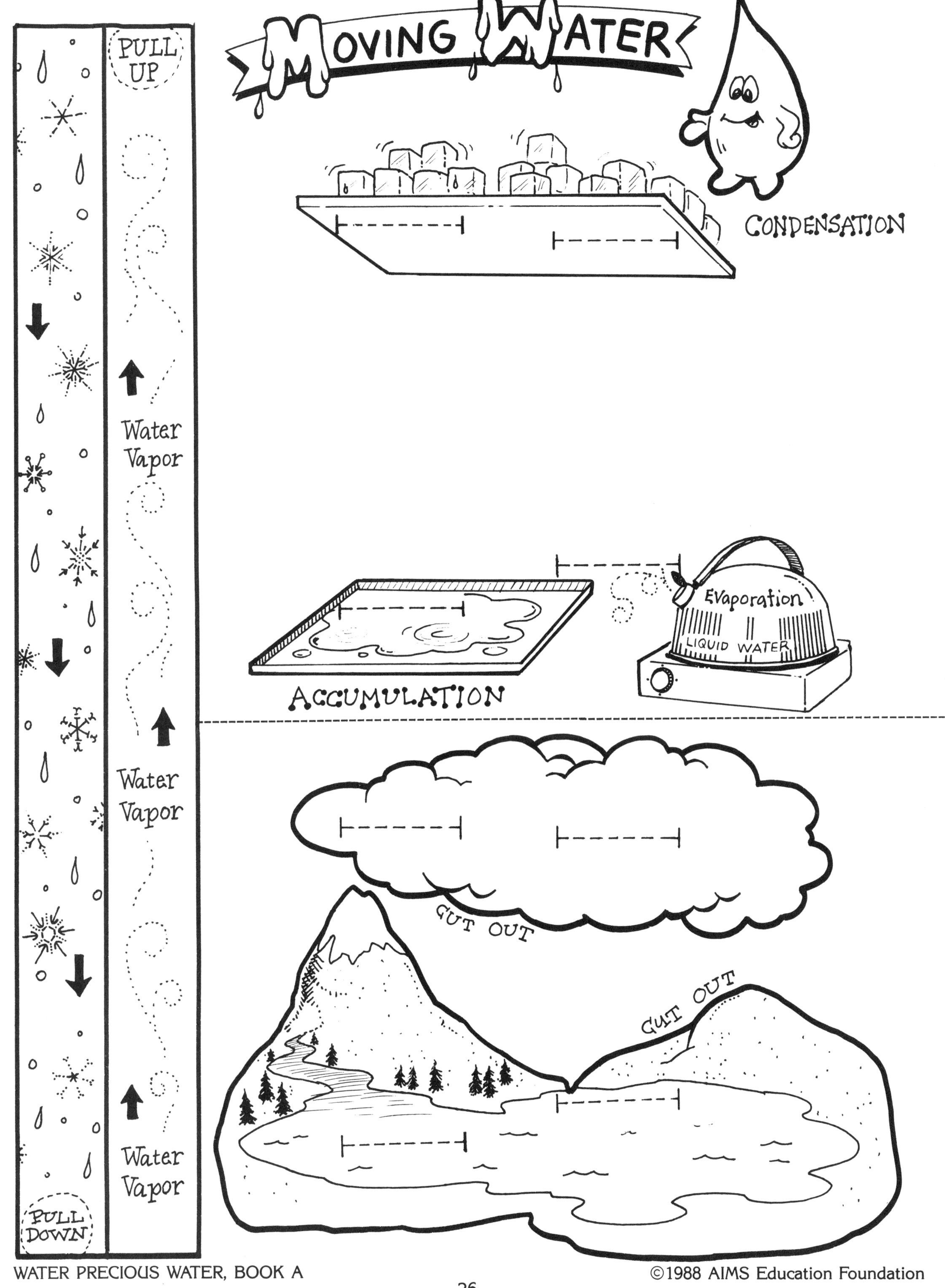
MOVING WATER
PULL UP
Water Vapor
Water Vapor
Water Vapor
PULL DOWN
CONDENSATION
Evaporation
LIQUID WATER
ACCUMULATION
CUT OUT
CUT OUT

MOVING RAINDROPS IN THE WATER CYCLE!

I. Topic Area
Water cycle

II. Introductory Statement
In this activity, students will construct a visual aid which depicts the water cycle.

III. Science Processes
a. Observation
b. Inference

IV. Materials
Per student:
2 dittos for water cycle wheel
1 paper fastener
crayons and scissors
1 tongue depressor or ice cream stick

V. Key Question
What different forms will water molecules go through as they move through the "water cycle"?

VI. Background Information
See background information on the water cycle in the "Moving Water" activity.

VII. Management Suggestions
Discuss the water cycle in nature and the terms evaporation, condensation, precipitation and accumulation. Use a picture of a typical water cycle from the student text or draw one on the board.

VIII. Procedure
1. Refer to the previous demonstration with the "teakettle" and review the words:
   a. evaporation — the changing of liquid water to a vapor or gas which is invisible.
   b. condensation — the changing of water vapor back to a liquid form (example: steam or clouds in nature).
2. Discuss how this same cycle also occurs on earth with *evaporation* of water from the ocean, lakes, and the earth's soil. The cooling of the water vapor called *condensation* forms clouds and fog. Review the terms precipitation and accumulation of water in lakes, rivers and streams and finally discuss how water moves down through the ground into the "ground water". Explain how some of the water eventually ends up in the ocean.
3. Show a picture of the water cycle in a text or draw a simple picture on the board. Continue to draw analogies between "Teakettle Demonstration" and the natural water cycle.
4. Stress that the *same* water molecule has gone through millions of changes over the years. The same water molecules that they drink today may have been in the Nile River or part of a glacier during the last Ice Age.
5. Demonstrate how the water moves through the cycle, changing form from a liquid to a solid or vapor, but still retaining the same molecular shape (explain molecular structure to older students).

What the Students Will Do:
1. Participate in a class discussion on water cycle.
2. Assemble and utilize "Water Cycle — Raindrop Wheel".
   Note: The wheel will be more durable if copied on heavy paper or tag. Tape the tongue depressor to the back of the top disk to act as a handle.

IX. Discussion
1. How many different changes does the liquid water in the ocean go through when moving through the water cycle? Describe the changes.
2. Is it possible for the same water molecule to be in a liquid, a vapor, and an ice crystal form while going through the phases of the water cycle?
3. What causes a solid to change to a liquid and then to a vapor or gas?
4. What causes a gas or vapor to change to a liquid and then a solid?
5. What would happen if the temperature never got above 32 °F or 0 °C? If the temperature never went below 32 °F or 0 °C, how would this affect life on earth?

X. Extensions
1. Try making a miniature water cycle by putting a closed jar, with a small amount of water in it, in a sunny location.
2. Place three jars in different temperature locations to note the different amounts of water vapor that collect in each jar.

Curriculum Coordinates:
1. Language Arts — Write a story written by a little rain drop or water molecule and explain where he's been or where he is going.

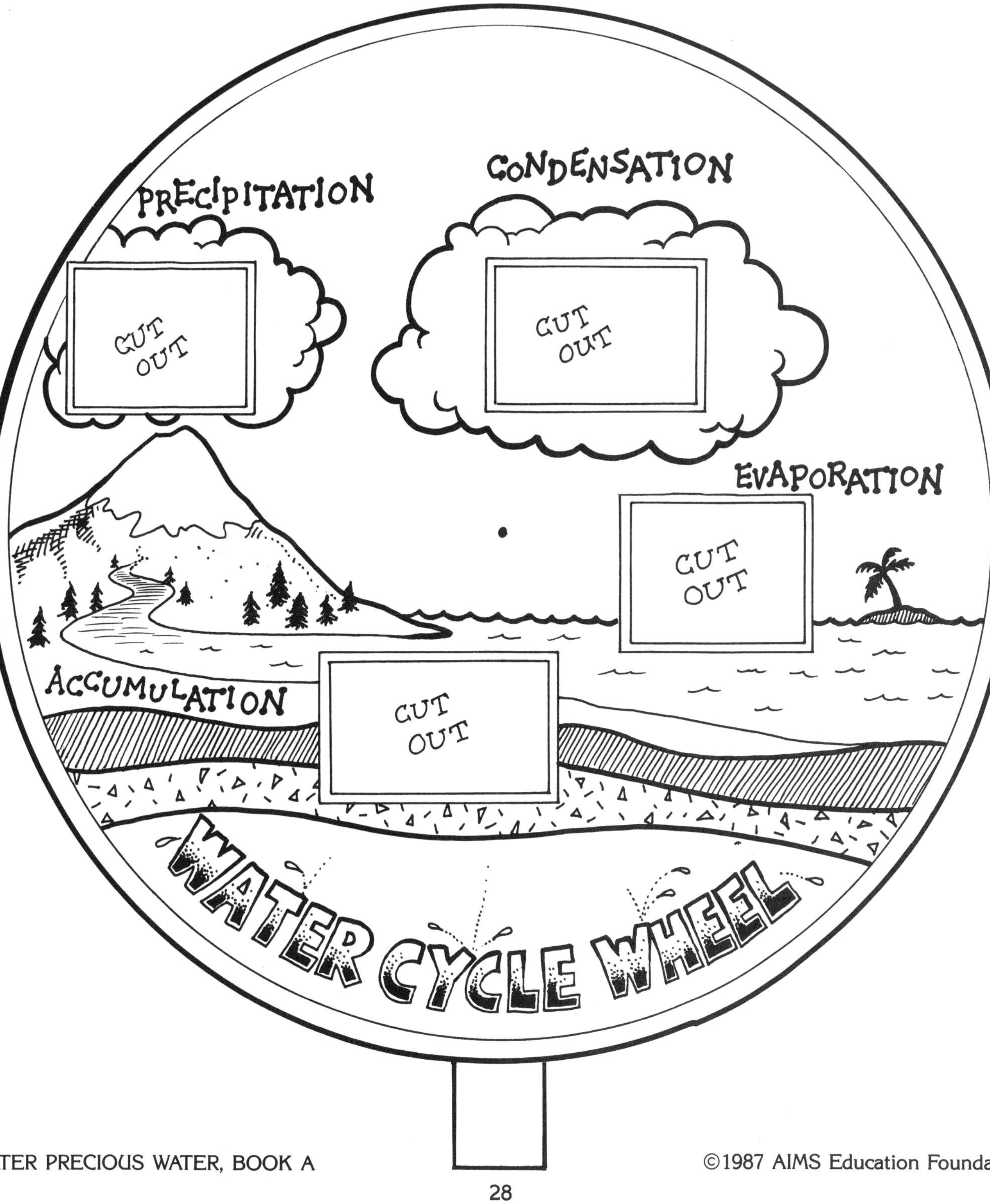

PRECIPITATION

CONDENSATION

CUT OUT

CUT OUT

EVAPORATION

CUT OUT

ACCUMULATION

CUT OUT

WATER CYCLE WHEEL

Moving Raindrops

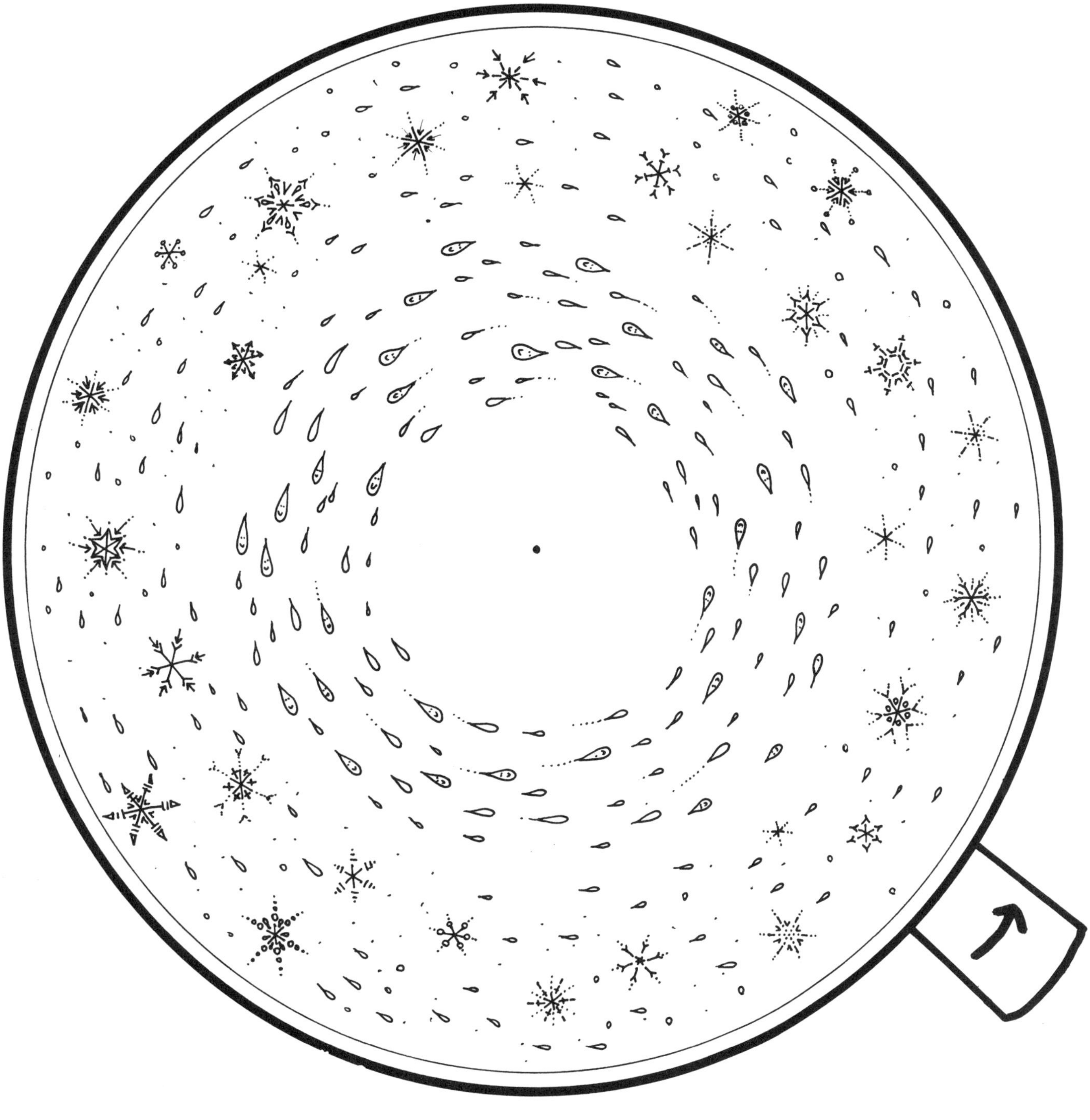

POND TODAY — MEADOW TOMORROW

I. Topic Area

Evaporation

II. Introductory Statement

This activity will show students how physical and biological processes interact to produce changes in the environment as they simulate a pond turning into a meadow as the water evaporates.

III. Math Skills	**Science Processes**
a. Counting	a. Classifying
b. Graphing	b. Predicting
c. Measuring	c. Collecting and recording data
	d. Controlling variables

IV. Materials

aquariums or large plastic containers
soil
rye grass seed or birdseed
three varieties of water plants
metric rulers
activity sheets

V. Key Question

What happens as an aquatic environment changes to a land environment?

VI. Background Information

Our environment is constantly changing as a result of the interaction between physical and biological processes. We call this change succession. It is a slow process that occurs continuously.

VII. Management Suggestions

This is a long term activity that will take approximately three weeks. A schedule should be set up that allows time to observe and record results every three days. This activity can be done in groups or as an entire class. Aquariums or large plastic containers work best for this activity, but two liter plastic bottles with the tops cut off will also work. The soil in the containers should be sloped, with part of the soil above the water line and part of the soil below the water line. Aquatic plants can be found at pet stores or anywhere that fish and aquariums are sold.

VIII. Procedure

1. Put a layer of soil in the container and make it slope steeply from one side of the container to the other. Add enough water so that half of the soil is above the water line and half is below.
2. Count out ten seeds and sprinkle them in the container. Some of the seeds may fall on the dry soil and some in the water.
3. Place three different aquatic plants in the water. Draw a picture on the activity sheet showing what the environment looks like.
4. Every three days sprinkle ten more seeds into the container.
5. Measure and record the water level. Do not add more water.
6. Count and record the total number of seeds that are growing. Check the three water plants and record whether they are alive or dead.
7. On days 5, 10 and 15 draw a picture of the environment on the activity sheet.

IX. Discussion Questions

1. Discuss the questions on the activity sheet.
2. How do seeds get spread in nature?
3. How would pollution change the environments?

X. Extended Activities

1. Make another pond environment and deliberately pollute it by adding things like salt, oil, soap, etc.
2. Allow all the water to evaporate and then add more water to simulate flooding. See what happens to the land plants as they are submerged for a period of time.

POND TODAY...MEADOW TOMORROW
DAY 1
DAY 5
draw what you see...
DAY 10
DAY 15

POND TODAY... MEADOW TOMORROW

Draw in the water level and any other changes you see.

DAY 1

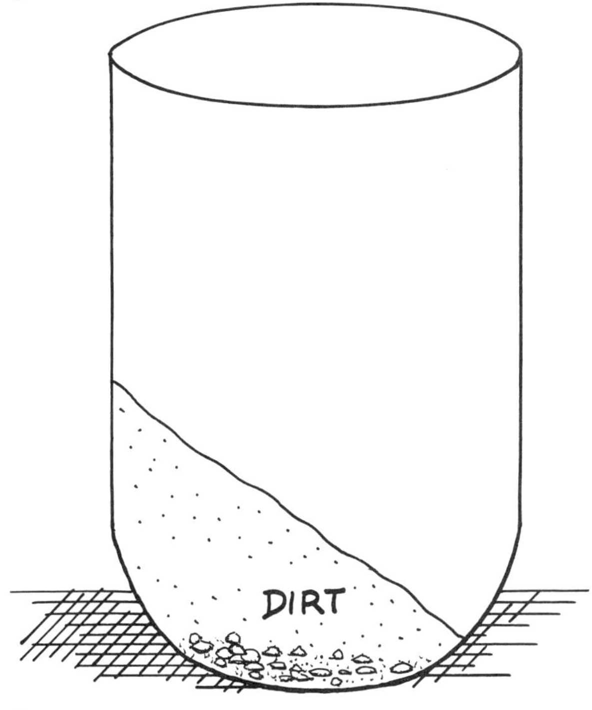

DAY 5

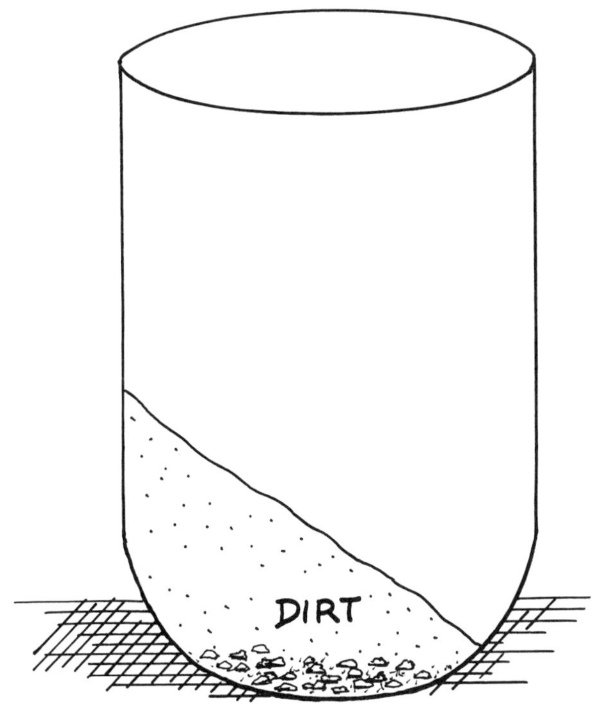

DAY 10

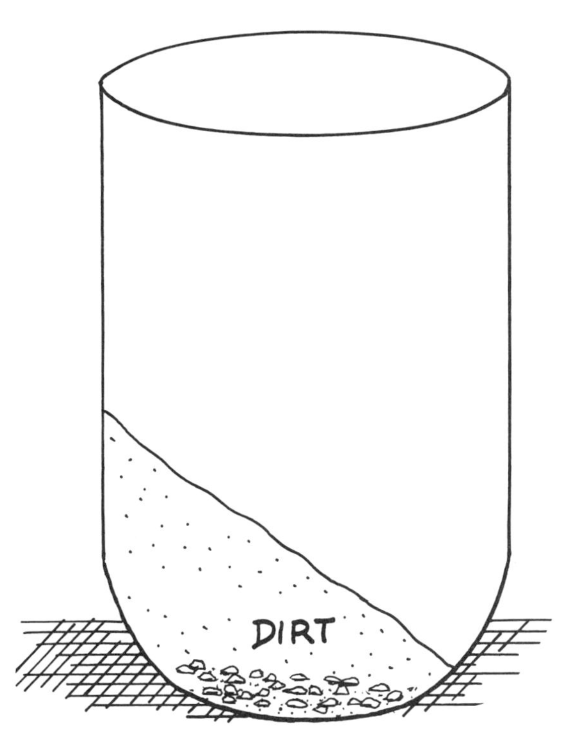

DAY 15

POND TODAY... MEADOW TOMORROW I

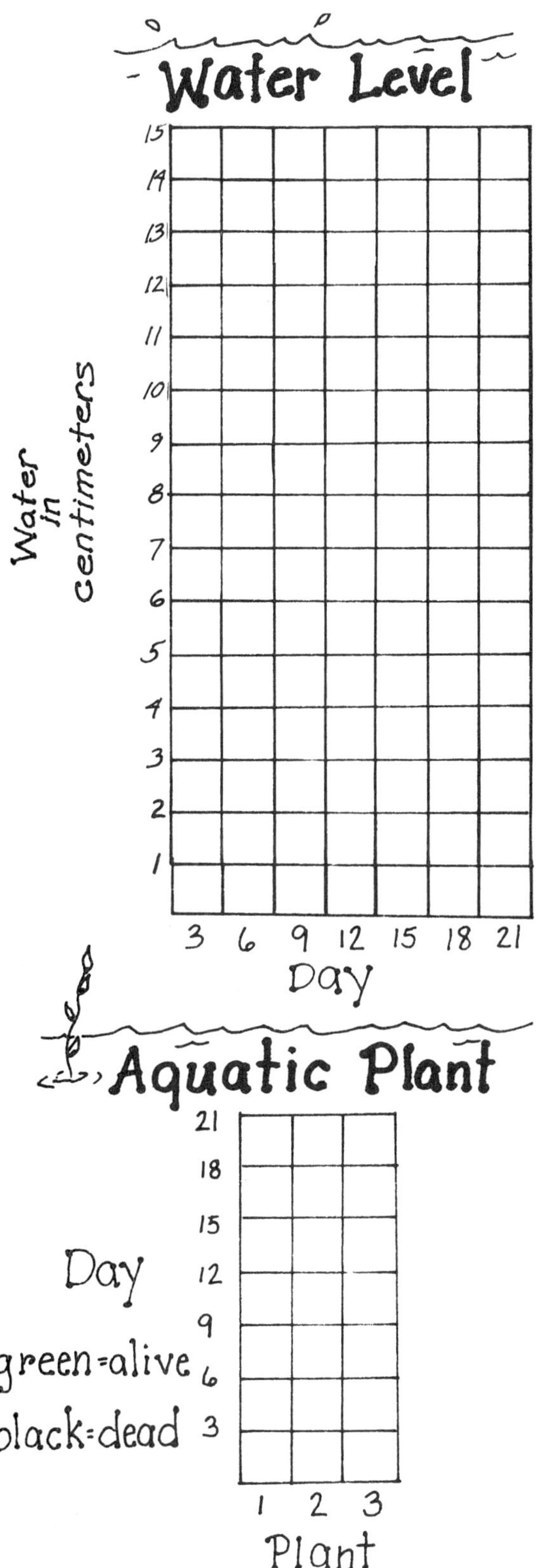

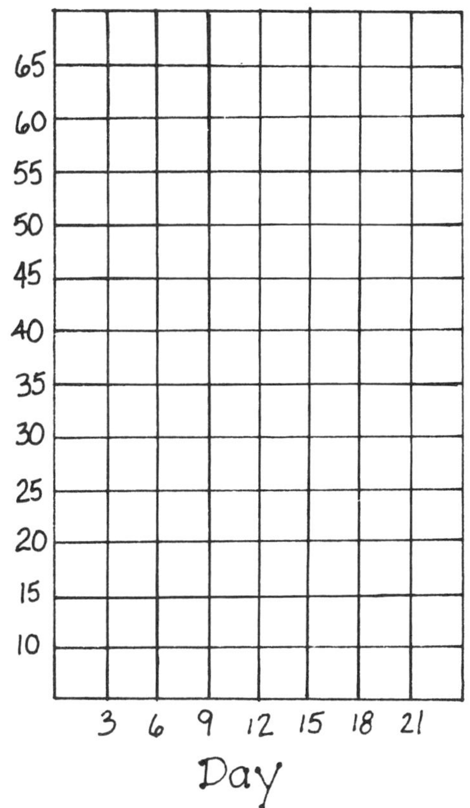

- What did you observe after all the water evaporated?
- Do you think the environment will change again? Explain...
- How does succession affect our water supply?
- How does rainfall affect succession?

MOVING MOLECULES

I. Topic Area
Water and evaporation

II. Introductory Statement
Students will determine if the amount of surface area will affect the evaporation rate of liquids.

III. Math Skills
a. Data gathering
b. Computation
c. Graphing
d. Measuring
e. Finding area

Science Processes
a. Hypothesizing
b. Controlling variables
c. Interpreting data
d. Drawing conclusions

IV. Materials
activity sheets
1 beaker or graduated cylinder per group
1 waterproof rectangular container per group
water
1 metric ruler per group

V. Key Question
How does the amount of surface area affect the rate of evaporation of water?

VI. Background Information
Water can exist in 3 forms; as a solid, a liquid, or a gas. Evaporation is the phase change of a liquid to a gas. This change is affected by several variables. The variables are temperature, air pressure, surface area, wind speed and density. This lesson measures the effect of surface area on evaporation rates. When water molecules evaporate, they break free from the surface of the water. The number of water molecules that are able to break free into the air is determined by the surface area of the water. The greater the surface area, the more opportunity for water molecules to break away as vapor.

VII. Management Suggestions
1. Collect enough containers beforehand so that each group will have one. The containers should be rectangular in shape with perpendicular sides. Try to get a different sized container for each group. The containers should not have tops and should be waterproof, otherwise they need to be lined with plastic wrap. You can use different sized milk cartons with the tops or sides cut off, baking pans, plastic boxes, tupperware, etc., for this activity.
2. This activity takes five days. More time, 30–45 minutes, will be spent on the first and last days, while the other days require only 5–15 minutes to measure and record data.
3. Divide the class into groups of 4–6 students. The activity page is set up for 6 groups.
4. Students should be able to measure the opening of their rectangular container and calculate its area by multiplying the length by the width. The area may also be found using centimeter grid paper and tracing the opening and then counting the squares.
5. The mass of the water can be used as a measure of evaporation instead of the volume. You will need a scale to do this.

VIII. Procedure
1. Divide the class into groups. Give each group a different sized container and a ruler or tape measure.
2. Have the groups find the area of the opening of their container. Write the areas on the board. Label the containers A,B,C,D and E, with A having the smallest opening and E having the largest. Each student should record this information on the activity sheet.
3. Distribute a beaker and water to each group.
4. Discuss the question on the activity sheet and have students make a hypothesis.
5. Each group will measure 250 ml of water and pour it into their container.
6. Put all of the containers on a counter top. Be sure that all of the containers are positioned so that other variables, such as wind or temperature do not affect the evaporation rate. If you would like a control group, get 2 of each container and cover 1 of them to show that placing a lid on the container will prevent evaporation.
7. Measure the volume of the water each day for 4 days and record it on the data chart. Each group will share their data so that all students can record it on their activity sheet.
8. On the last day use the data in the total evaporated column and complete the bar graph on the second activity sheet. Students can also make a line graph to see the relationship between surface area and evaporation.
9. Have the students discuss the graph and write conclusions about the relationship between surface area and evaporation rates.
10. Error analysis. Have the students discuss other variables that could have affected the results. Discuss ways to have more accurately measured the water.

IX. Discussion Questions
1. How does surface area affect evaporation?
2. What other variables other than surface area affect evaporation rates?
3. How could you use the information from this activity to estimate how much water evaporates daily from a swimming pool?

X. Extended Activities
1. Repeat this experiment with other liquids.
2. Use circular or other shaped containers and use centimeter grid paper to find the surface area.
3. Use the depth of the water to measure amount of evaporation.
4. Calculate the surface area of a swimming pool and use your findings to estimate how much water is lost to evaporation.

Moving Molecules

Name ____________________

Question: Does the area of the opening of a container affect the rate at which water will evaporate?

Hypothesis: ________________________________

Area → [____ cm.] width of opening × [____ cm] length of opening = [____ cm^2] area of opening

H_2O

H_2O

H_2O

Data Gathering:

container	(L×W) Area of opening	Volume of Water in Milliliters: Day 1	Day 2	Day 3	Day 4	Day 5	A Beginning Volume	− B Ending Volume	= C Total Evaporated
A	cm^2						250 ml		
B	cm^2						250 ml		
C	cm^2						250 ml		
D	cm^2						250 ml		
E	cm^2						250 ml		
F	cm^2						250 ml		

Moving Molecules

Graph the total water evaporated.

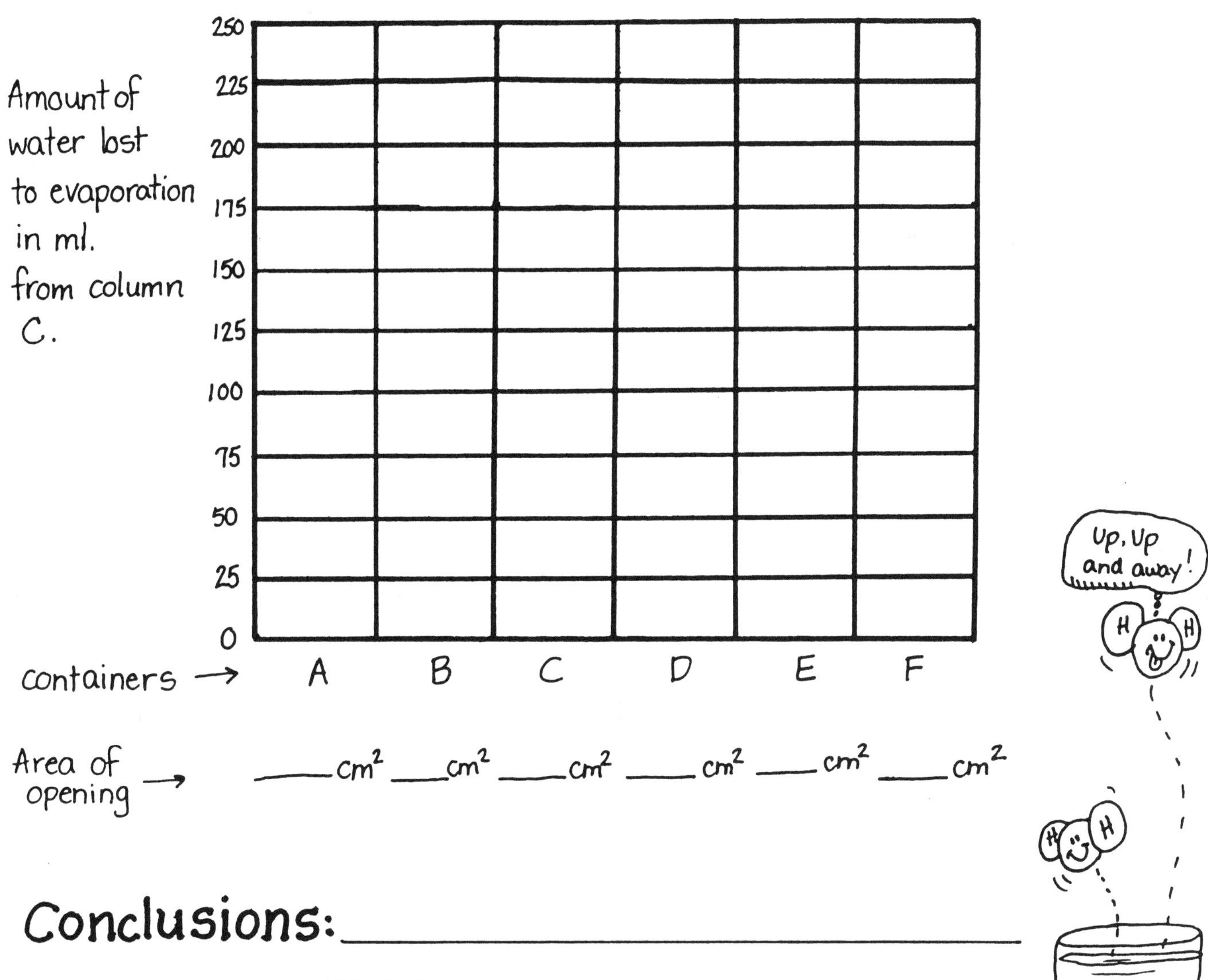

Conclusions: ______________________________

____

____

Error Analysis: What would be a better way to test this variable? ______________________________

____

____

The Effect of Surface Area on Evaporation

Choose a color to represent each container and fill in the key. Construct a line graph.

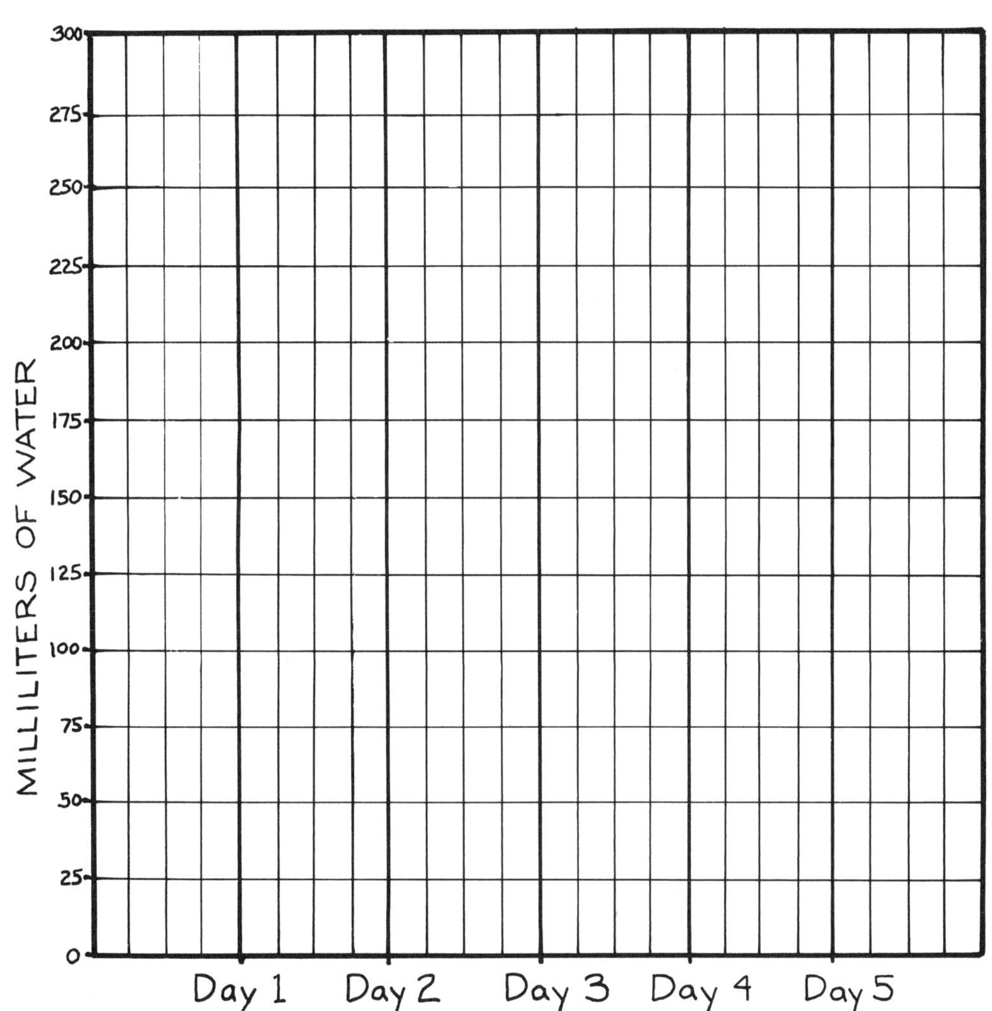

What does the completed graph tell you?

____

____

____

____

DOWN THE DRAIN

I. Topic Area

Water conservation

II. Introductory Statement

Students will measure the amount of water wasted when allowing a spigot to run until the water gets warm.

III. Math Skills

a. Whole number operations
b. Averaging
c. Projecting data
d. Measuring

Science Processes

a. Predicting
b. Estimating
c. Collecting and analyzing data

IV. Materials

large bucket
watch or clock
liter measuring container
activity sheet

V. Key Question

How much water is wasted while waiting for the water in the hot water tap to become warm?

VI. Background Information

As the population of a community grows the demand for water increases. Conservation of water is a vital aspect for present and future considerations. One way in which water is wasted is by running the tap until the water gets warm. Students will measure the amount of water wasted while waiting for it to get warm and then project their results onto a larger sample of water users. Many hot water tanks are located far from the point of use. Locating the tank nearer to the sinks would decrease the amount of water being wasted.

VII. Management Suggestions

1. Use "Down the Drain I" as a homework assignment and introductory activity.
2. Locate a sink with a hot water tap at your school for collecting the data for "Down the Drain II".
3. Be sure the tap is cool before beginning. Wait a few minutes if someone has recently used it.
4. Use an almanac to find the populations of cities, states, and country.
5. Use calculators to compute the projections in "Down the Drain II".

VIII. Procedure

1. Begin by discussing the questions on the first student page. Have students do "Down the Drain I" for homework. Discuss the results of this activity before doing "Down the Drain II."
2. Pass out the "Down the Drain II" activity sheet. Discuss and have students predict how many liters will be wasted in trial 1.
3. Put a pail under a hot water faucet. Be sure that the water has not been run for at least 10 minutes. Turn on the faucet and collect the water until the water becomes warm. As soon as the water becomes slightly warm run the tap for 5 more seconds and stop.
4. Take the collected sample to the classroom and measure the amount in liters.
5. Repeat procedure #3 for trials 2 and 3. Be sure that the water is cool in the tap before beginning each trial. Have the students predict the amount of water wasted prior to each trial.
6. Compute the average amount of water wasted.
7. Assume that a similar amount of water is wasted daily by each person in your city, state and country.
8. Using the above assumption complete the projections section of the activity sheet. Use calculators if available.
9. Discuss ways to solve this problem. Contact the local water company as a resource.

IX. Discussion Questions

1. How could the wasted water have been used?
2. How might this problem be solved?
3. How much water would be wasted in 10 years?

X. Extended Activities

1. Repeat the activity with the amount of water wasted letting the tap run while brushing your teeth. Compare this to using a cup of water. See the lesson "A Little Cup Will Do It."
2. Repeat the activity at home and compare the amount wasted from various homes. Use "Down the Drain I" activity sheet.
3. Create water conservation posters.
4. Repeat the activity with the amount of water wasted while waiting for the tap to get cold.

Please... Don't Waste Me!

Down the Drain I

Questions

- How much time does it take for the hot water spigot to turn warm?
- How much water was wasted?

Test #1: Test the kitchen sink — How long did it take for the water to turn warm?

Time:		Amount of Water (opt.)	
Prediction	______	Prediction	________
Actual	______	Actual	________

Test #2: Test the bathroom sink — How long did it take for the water to turn warm?

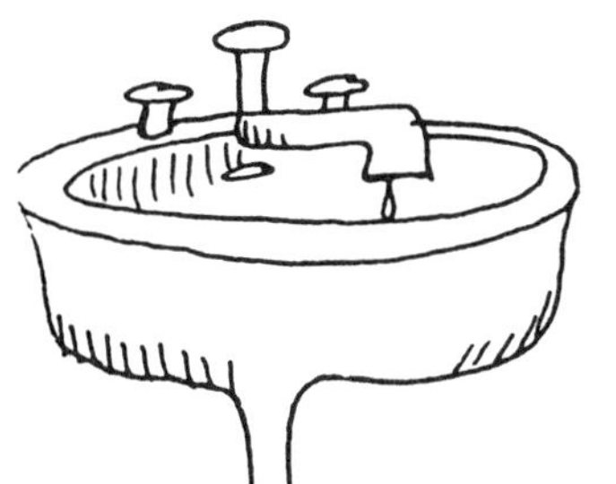

Time:		Amount of Water (opt.)	
Prediction	______	Prediction	________
Actual	______	Actual	________

Is there a difference between the kitchen sink and the bathroom sink? ______________

If so, why? ______________________

____

____

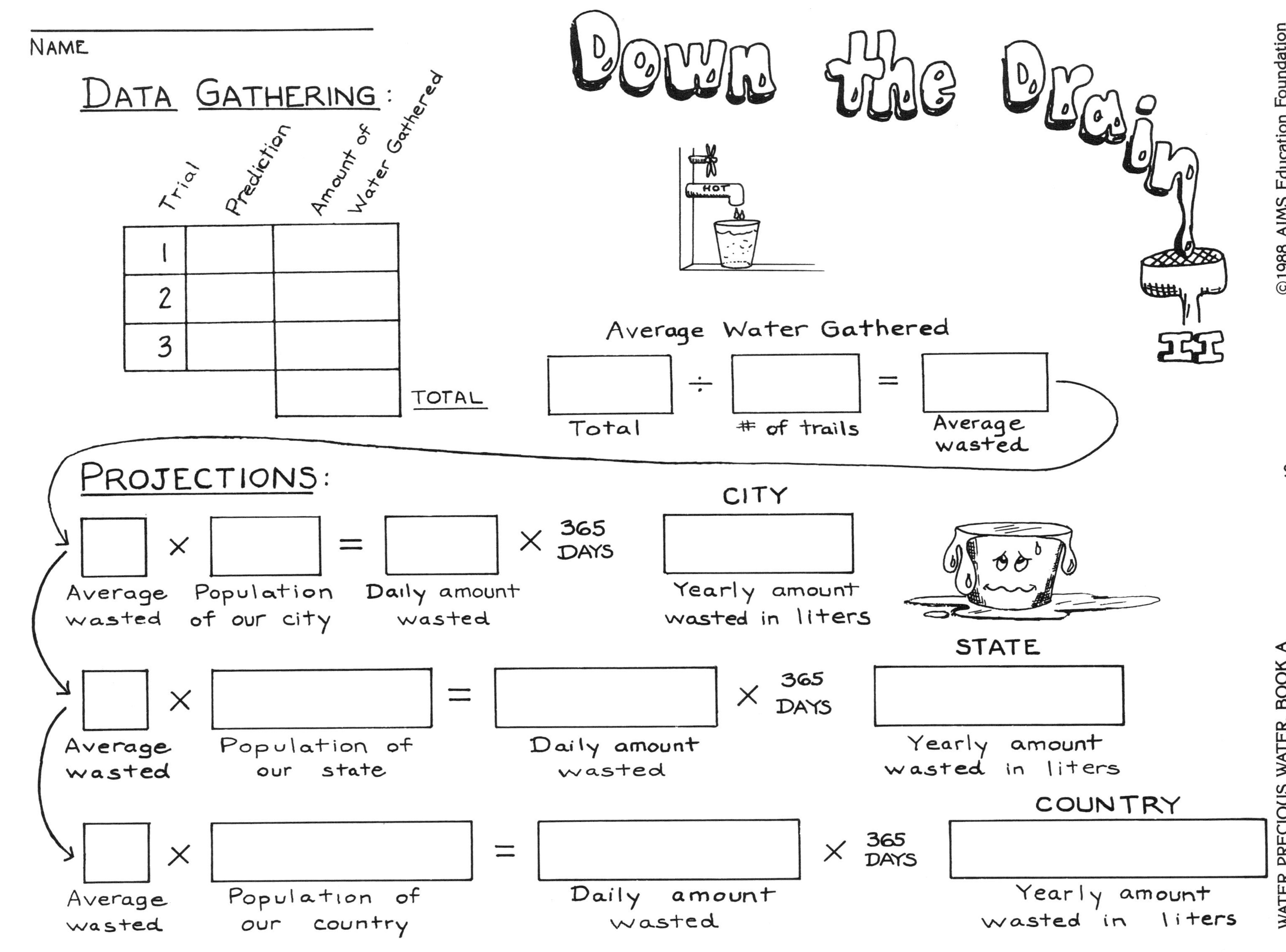
NAME
Down the Drain II
DATA GATHERING:
Trial
Prediction
Amount of Water Gathered
1
2
3
TOTAL
HOT
Average Water Gathered
Total
÷
# of trails
=
Average wasted
PROJECTIONS:
CITY
Average wasted
×
Population of our city
=
Daily amount wasted
× 365 DAYS
Yearly amount wasted in liters
STATE
Average wasted
×
Population of our state
=
Daily amount wasted
× 365 DAYS
Yearly amount wasted in liters
COUNTRY
Average wasted
×
Population of our country
=
Daily amount wasted
× 365 DAYS
Yearly amount wasted in liters

DRIP DROP FLIP FLOP

I. Topic Area

Water conservation

II. Introductory Statement

Students will play a game in which they will identify ways water is being wasted and how water can be conserved.

III. Science Processes

a. Observing
b. Classifying
c. Organizing data
d. Hypothesizing

IV. Materials

activity sheets
butcher paper
crayons
scissors

V. Key Question

What are some ways to conserve water around your house?

VI. Background Information

There are many ways water is wasted around the home. A slowly leaking faucet can waste around 15 gallons a day. Waiting for the water to get hot can waste 5 to 10 gallons. A fifteen minute shower uses about 120 gallons. Letting the faucet run while brushing your teeth wastes a gallon of water. This activity will help students see ways that water is wasted around the home and help them become more aware of ways they can help conserve water.

VII. Management Suggestions

1. Prepare the game cards beforehand or allow time for the students to cut them out.
2. Use the butcher paper to make a town with streets and spaces for houses. The town can be divided into two sections, one for water wasters (the Drip family and their friends) and one for water savers (the Save-it family and their friends).
3. Divide your class into teams of two.

VIII. Procedure

1. Each team gets a set of 18 game cards which can be cut from the activity sheets.
2. Teams play memory by placing the game cards face down and trying to match a water wasting card with its corresponding water saving card.
3. Give each student a copy of the activity sheet depicting the house.
4. One student in each team will fill in the spaces by gluing on water saving cards or drawing in pictures showing wise uses of water and the other will do the same showing water being wasted.
5. The students will then cut out their houses and glue them on the butcher paper town in the appropriate areas, either on the side with the Drip family or on the side with the Save-it family.

XI. Discussion

1. How can you save water at home?
2. How can you help your family keep from wasting water?
3. What water wasting is going on at school and how can it be prevented?
4. What can your class do to help your community become better conservers of water?

X. Extensions

1. Have your students act as water consultants. Have them write a letter to the Drip family explaining how they can help conserve water.
2. Have the students draw additional sets of cards for the game.
3. Make posters promoting water conservation and put them up around the school or community.

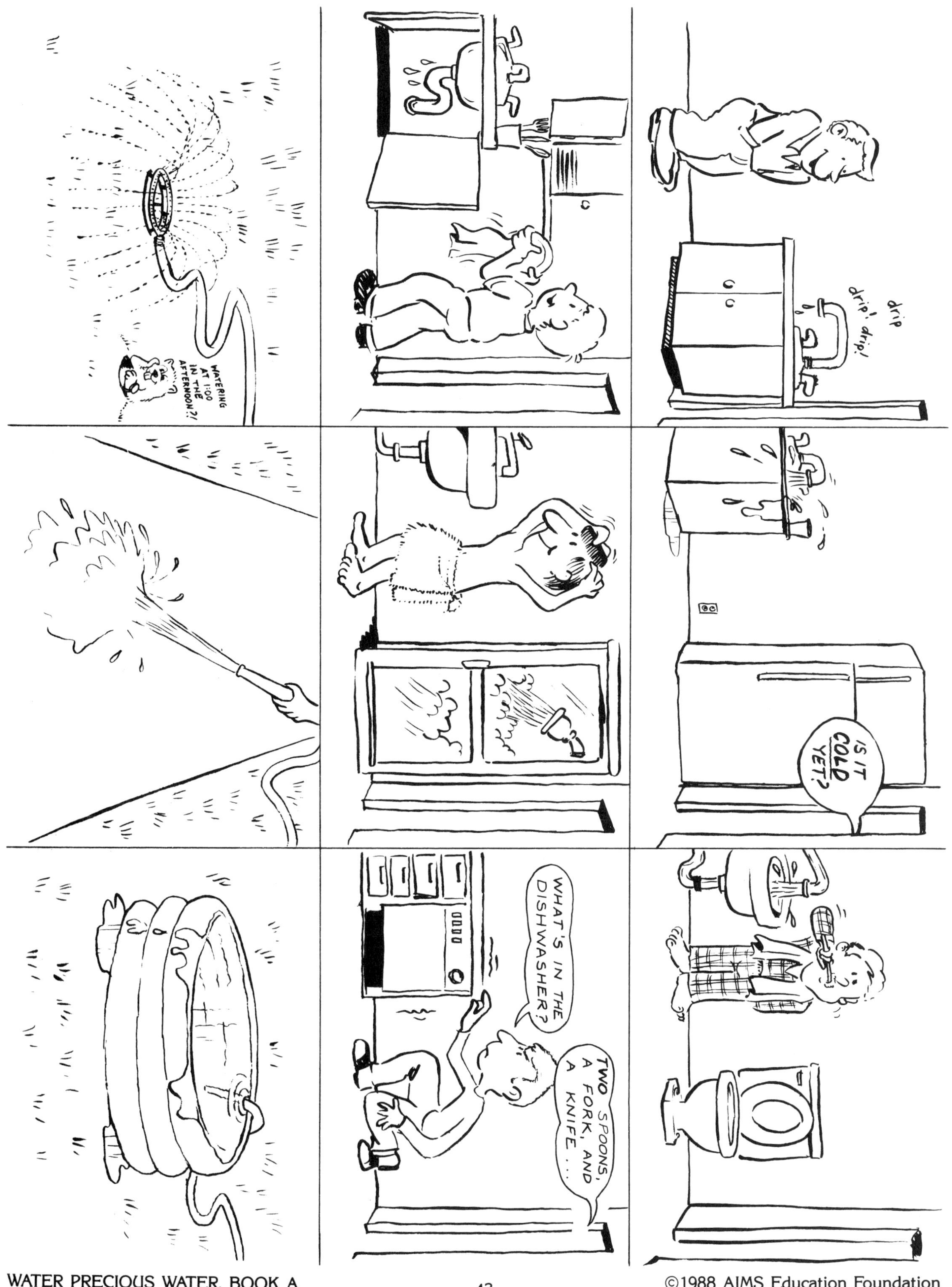
drip
drip! drip!
IS IT COLD YET?
WHAT'S IN THE DISHWASHER?
TWO SPOONS, A FORK, AND A KNIFE . . .
WATERING AT 1:00 IN THE AFTERNOON?!

WHAT'S IN THE DISHWASHER?
ALL THE BREAKFAST, LUNCH, AND DINNER DISHES.
MY AFTERNOON NAP

A LITTLE CUP WILL DO IT

I. Topic Area
Water conservation

II. Introductory Statement
This activity will show students how they can conserve large quantities of water just by changing the way they brush their teeth.

III. Math Skills	**Science Processes**
a. Computation	a. Observing
b. Measuring	b. Measuring
c. Estimating	c. Collecting and recording data
d. Predicting	d. Inferring
	e. Applying and generalizing

IV. Materials
1 plastic cup per student
1 calibrated strip to match the cup used (see activity) "Make Your Own Measuring Cup"
1 activity sheet per student

V. Key Question
How much water can be saved in one week when brushing your teeth by using a cup of water instead of letting the water run?

VI. Background Information
Many people allow the tap to run while brushing their teeth. On a daily basis this uses about two gallons of water or 7.7 liters. This is based on using a gallon of water at each brushing, a.m. and p.m. In one week the water used to brush teeth while the tap is running totals 14 gallons, over 50 liters, for each individual. Projected on a yearly basis a person would use about 730 gallons or about 2,800 liters of water while brushing his/her teeth with the tap running. As water becomes scarce we must conserve this valuable resource. This lesson is designed to increase student awareness of ways to conserve water.

VII. Management Suggestions
1. This lesson is to be done at home. The students monitor their own use of water for 1 week.
2. Give each student a calibrated cup strip to tape to an appropriate paper or plastic cup. See "Make Your Own Measuring Cup" included in this book.
3. Discuss this lesson on a Friday and have students begin their data gathering on the next Monday morning.

VIII. Procedure
1. Discuss water and its importance to living things.
2. Discuss conservation of water. List ways of conserving.
3. Pass out the activity sheet "A Little Cup Will Do It."
4. Discuss the fact that most people allow the tap to run while brushing their teeth and people usually use 7,680 ml of water to brush twice a day.
5. Tell the students that they are going to be water savers and they are to brush their teeth using a cup of water (240 ml).
6. Give each student a calibrated cup.
7. Instruct the students to measure the amount of water they use while brushing their teeth each a.m. and p.m. while using a cup of water (240 ml).
8. Discuss the student activity sheet. Be sure the students take their cup and activity sheets home with them to gather data.
9. After 7 days of data is gathered, have the students total the amounts they used this week and also total the amount saved. Have the students pair up to verify each others computation.

IX. Discussion Questions
1. Why is it important to conserve water?
2. How could each person help to save water?
3. How much water would be saved if everyone in our school used a cup of water to brush their teeth?
4. What should we do now that our experiment is over?

X. Extended Activities
1. Upper grade students may complete the "A Little Cup Will Do It — Class Sheet". This activity is designed to project the total amount of water that a class may be able to save on a daily, monthly, and yearly basis.
2. Discuss ways to get other people involved in the "A Little Cup Will Do It" campaign.
3. Make posters about water conservation.
4. Upper grade students may calculate the total number of liters saved by dividing the total number of ml saved by 1,000.

A Little Cup Will Do It!

Task: Use less water while brushing your teeth.

Usual amount of water used = 1 gallon or 3.8 liters or 3,840 ml when the tap is running each time you brush your teeth.

New amount to be used = 1 cup or 240 ml.

Day	Water used in A.M.	Water used in P.M.	Total I used TODAY	Total I would have used today	Total I used TODAY	Total I SAVED
Mon.		+	= ____ ml.	7,680 ml.	– ____ ml.	=
Tues.		+	= ____ ml.	7,680 ml.	– ____ ml.	=
Wed.		+	= ____ ml.	7,680 ml.	– ____ ml.	=
Thurs.		+	= ____ ml.	7,680 ml.	– ____ ml.	=
Fri.		+	= ____ ml.	7,680 ml.	– ____ ml.	=
Sat.		+	= ____ ml.	7,680 ml.	– ____ ml.	=
Sun.		+	= ____ ml.	7,680 ml.	– ____ ml.	=
				Total used this week →		

Total ml. of water I saved this week ↑

1 gal. 3,840 ml   240 ml

*** Extra**

Total ml of water saved this week: ________ ml ÷ 1,000 ml = ______ → Total number of liters saved this week

A Little Cup Will Do It!

Save water while you brush your teeth.

Some boys and girls use a gallon (16 cups) of water because the tap is running when they brush their teeth. **YOU** can save water while brushing your teeth, if you use a cup of water instead of letting the water run.

Fill in the chart by coloring the amount you used when brushing your teeth:

	Monday	Tuesday	Wednesday	Thursday	Friday	Saturday	Sunday
A.M.	cup gallon	cup gallon	cup gallon	cup gallon	cup gallon	cup gallon	cup gallon
P.M.	cup gallon	cup gallon	cup gallon	cup gallon	cup gallon	cup gallon	cup gallon

I used ______ gallons of water.

I used ______ cups of water.

____
Name

A Little Cup Will Do It - Class Sheet

Total ml saved for class per day:

________ ml × ________ = ________ ml

Total number of ml of water saved by each student × Total number of students in class = Total number of ml saved by the whole class.

+

Total liters saved per class per day:

________ ÷ 1000 ml = ________

Total number of ml saved by class ÷ 1000 ml = Total number of liters saved by the class.

+

Total liters saved per class per month:

________ × 30 days = ________

Total number of liters saved per class per day. × Days = Total number of liters saved per class per month.

=

Total liters saved per class per year:

________ × 12 = ________

Total number of liters saved per class per month × months = Total number of liters saved per class per year

"Save today's water for tomorrow!"

WATER CLOCK — SHOWER TIMER

I. Topic Area
Water conservation

II. Introductory Statement
The students will construct and calibrate a water clock to be used as a "shower timer" to help them take shorter showers.

III. Math Skills
a. Measuring
b. Graphing
c. Calibrating

Science Processes
a. Observing
b. Measuring
c. Collecting and recording data
d. Controlling variables

IV. Materials
Per student:
- 1 soft, flexible, clear plastic cup or tumbler, 6 or 10 ounce size
- 1 calibrated milliliter strip from the lesson "Make Your Own Measuring Cup" to match the plastic cup
- 4 small paper clips
- 1 push pin
- 4 pieces of string 30 cm (12 in.) long
- 1 large bowl or bucket for the water to drain into while timing

V. Key Question
How many holes are needed in the bottom of a plastic cup to allow 240 ml of water to drain in 3 to 4 minutes?

VI. Background Information
During the next several years, water conservation will become a very important issue. Over 50% of all residential water usage occurs inside the home. Approximately 30% of that water usage comes under the category of "personal hygiene" that includes, baths, showers, and tooth brushing. A typical low-flow shower uses approximately 3 gallons of water per minute, while a normal shower head uses about 8 gallons per minute. A tub bath uses approximately 24 gallons. Therefore, an eight minute low-flow shower or a four minute regular shower use the same amount of water as a tub bath.

In this lesson, students will make their own calibrated cup to use as a shower timer. Each group will experiment with a plastic cup with 1 to 4 holes in the bottom of it. A calibrated paper strip to match the size of the cup should be cut out and taped to the outside of the cup. Refer to the activity, "Make Your Own Measuring Cup". This calibrated strip will enable the students to observe the number of milliliters of water drained from the cup per minute. The students should notice that the water leaves the cup more quickly during the first minute because the greater the depth of water, the greater the water pressure, therefore the water is forced through the holes at a faster rate.

As the water level is lowered, there is less water pressure pushing on the remaining water in the cup, slowing the rate of flow. The cup does not completely empty because the minimal amount of water left in the cup covers the holes and surface tension prevents the water from completely dripping out.

Four push pin holes in the bottom of the 6 ounce tumbler cause it to drain in about 3½ to 4 minutes. A three to four minute regular shower is equal in water usage to a tub bath, so the above "water clock" would be a reliable timer for conserving water while showering.

Note: Different size cups will produce different flow rates depending on the depth of the column of water remaining in the cup as well as the number of holes in the bottom.

VIII. Procedure
1. Pass out 1 cup per student and assign each student in a group of 4 to make either 1, 2, 3 or 4 holes in the bottom of their cup with a push pin. Each person in the group should have a different number of holes in their cup.
2. Poke 4 equally spaced holes under the rim of the cup and insert 1 small paper clip into each hole.
3. Tie the 4 pieces of string to the paper clips and make a hanger so the cup can be hung in the shower.
4. Pass out one calibrated strip to match the cup to each student and have them tape it onto their cup.
5. Pass out the activity sheet and discuss the purpose and procedures to be used in this experiment with the class.
6. Model how to fill the cup and place it over a bowl or bucket to catch the water as it drains and record the *remaining* milliliters of water per minute until the dripping almost stops.
7. The students will time the water flow for their cups until the dripping almost stops or slows dramatically. This time can be rounded to the nearest minute or half minute. There will always be a small amount of water left in the cup.
8. Have the students record their own times on the activity sheet and share the results with each member of their group.
9. Each student will then compute the average rate of water flow per minute for each cup in the group and complete the graph.
10. Students will compute how many gallons of water they would use in a regular shower if they used their cup as a shower timer.
11. Discuss the results of this activity. Tell students that a normal shower uses about 8 gallons of water a minute while a low-flow shower uses about 3 gallons a minute and a tub bath about 24 gallons. Have students calculate the amount of time a normal and low-flow shower can run to use the same amount of water as a bath. Students can then select the appropriate water clock to use as a timer for their shower.
12. Encourage the students to take the water clock home and use it in the shower to time their showers. They can tie the full cup of water to the shower head. When the cup is almost empty or drips very slowly, their shower is over!

IX. Discussion Questions
1. Discuss why it is important to conserve water by limiting the amount of water used in showering.
2. Help students to compute the amount of water used on a 5, 8 and 10 minute shower. Compute the amount of water saved in each of these examples if they took a 4 minute shower instead.

X. Extended Activities
1. Have the students research the "water clock" as an ancient method of timekeeping.
2. Have the students compute how many milliliters of water they should put into their cups (with less than 4 holes) to have it empty in 3 minutes.
3. Brainstorm other methods of personal water conservation that may be practiced or devices that could be made to help save water.

XI. Curriculum Coordinates
1. Social Studies: Research ancient time-keeping devices.
2. Math: Compute different rates of water flow using different height cups.

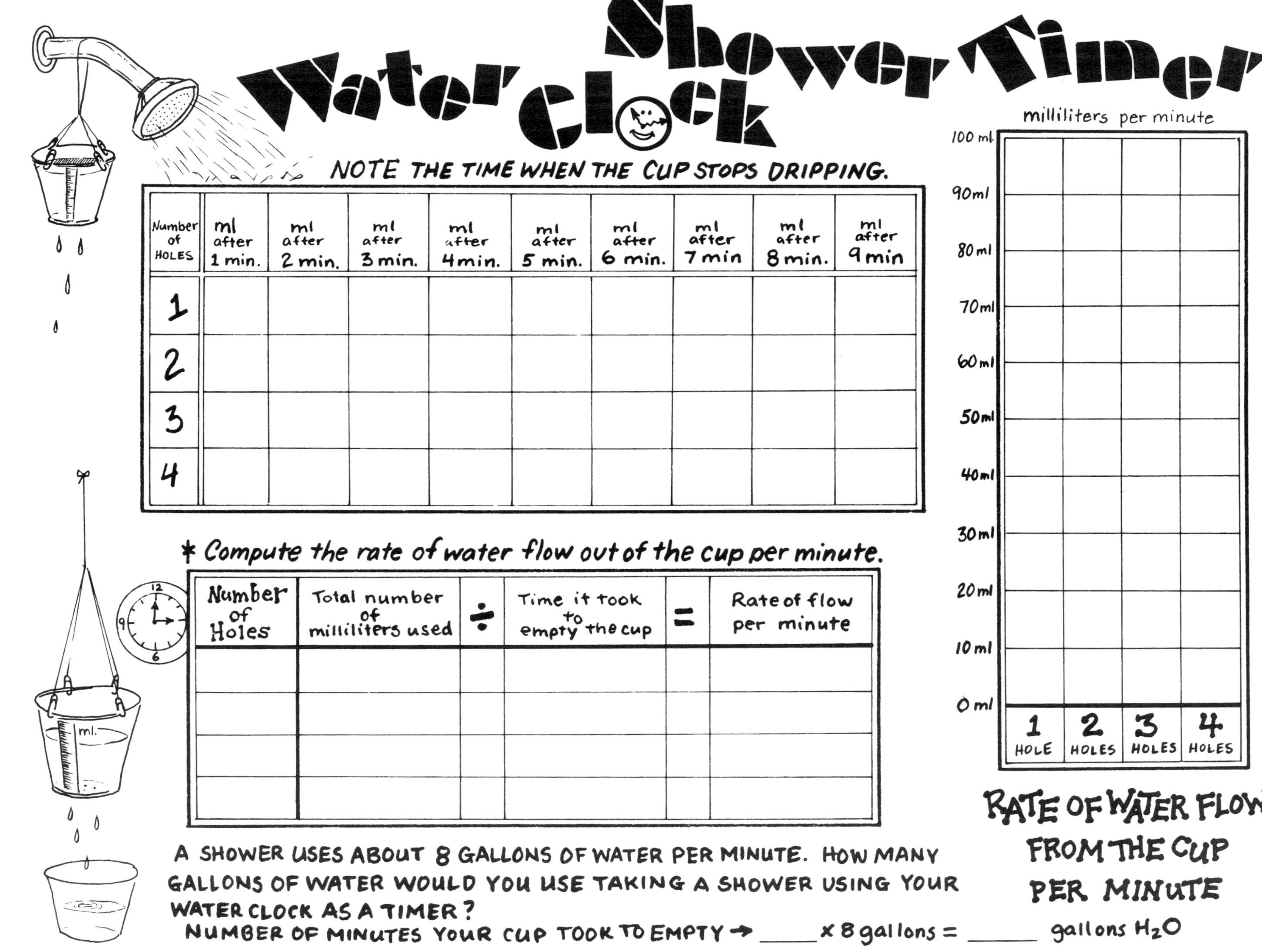

Water Clock Shower Timer

NOTE THE TIME WHEN THE CUP STOPS DRIPPING.

Number of HOLES	ml after 1 min.	ml after 2 min.	ml after 3 min.	ml after 4 min.	ml after 5 min.	ml after 6 min.	ml after 7 min	ml after 8 min.	ml after 9 min
1									
2									
3									
4									

* Compute the rate of water flow out of the cup per minute.

Number of Holes	Total number of milliliters used	÷	Time it took to empty the cup	=	Rate of flow per minute

RATE OF WATER FLOW FROM THE CUP PER MINUTE

A SHOWER USES ABOUT 8 GALLONS OF WATER PER MINUTE. HOW MANY GALLONS OF WATER WOULD YOU USE TAKING A SHOWER USING YOUR WATER CLOCK AS A TIMER?

NUMBER OF MINUTES YOUR CUP TOOK TO EMPTY → ____ × 8 gallons = ____ gallons H_2O

THAT SETTLES IT!

I. Topic Area

Water treatment — settling

II. Introductory Statement

This activity will demonstrate the process of settling, an important step in the treatment of water.

III. Math Skills

a. Measuring mass
b. Measuring volume

Science Processes

a. Predicting
b. Observing
c. Comparing
d. Interpreting
e. Generalizing

IV. Materials

Per team:
- calibrated cup
- clear testing jar with a lid and straight sides
- vegetable oil
- clean sand
- scales and gram weights
- food coloring
- centimeter ruler
- water

V. Key Question

How can settling be used to clean water that is dirty?

VI. Background Information

A mixture is a combination of substances in which the parts can be separated. Settling is one method of separating a mixture of liquids and solids. When a mixture of liquids and solids settles, some material sinks to the bottom and some floats to the top. Settling is the first step in the water treatment process. Layering will occur due to the differing densities of the materials. The bottom layers will be the most dense and the top layers the least dense.

VII. Management Suggestions

1. Divide class into teams.
2. Suggested types of jars to use as testing jars; canning jars, peanut butter jars or jam jars.
3. If clean sand is not available, rinse sand and pour off the dirty water, repeating the process as often as necessary.

VIII. Procedure

1. Show the students the 3 items (oil, water, sand) to be poured into jar.
2. Draw a picture in the first jar of how they think it will look after pouring in the 3 items.

What the Students will do:

1. Measure 100 ml of water using the calibrated measuring cup and pour it into the testing jar.
2. Add 2 drops of food coloring to water.
3. Measure 100 ml of vegetable oil using the calibrated measuring cup and pour it into the testing jar.
4. Use scales to weigh out 50 grams of clean sand and add it to the testing jar.
5. Draw a picture in the second jar on the activity sheet showing what the mixture looks like after pouring but before shaking.
6. Use a centimeter ruler, measure and record the height of the water.
7. Predict what the jar will look like 10 minutes after shaking. Draw a picture in the third jar on the activity sheet showing your predictions.
8. Draw a picture in the fourth jar on the activity sheet showing what the mixture looks like immediately after shaking.
9. Allow the mixture to settle for about 10 minutes. Complete the activity sheet by drawing what the jar looks like after settling in the last jar on the activity sheet.

IX. Discussion Questions

1. Why could this mixture be called a chemistry sandwich?
2. Why did the layering of materials occur?
3. Why would this method be used in the process of cleaning our drinking water?
4. What happened to the height of the water before and after shaking?

X. Extended Activities

1. Students could experiment with other mixtures.
2. Give students a dirty water mixture for them to clean by applying their newly gained knowledge on settling.
3. Do the activity "Help Save the Dirty Birds" in this book.

THAT SETTLES IT

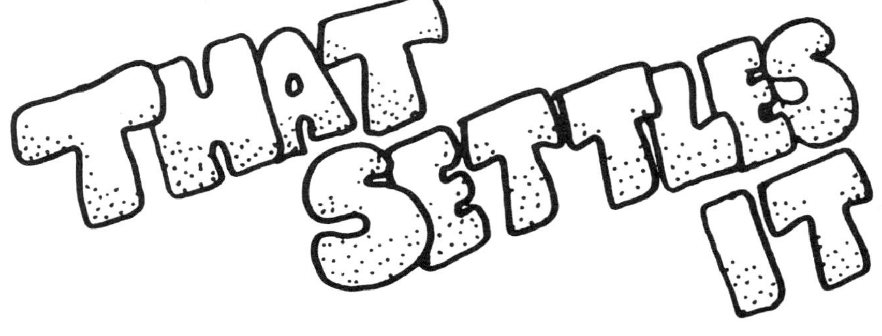

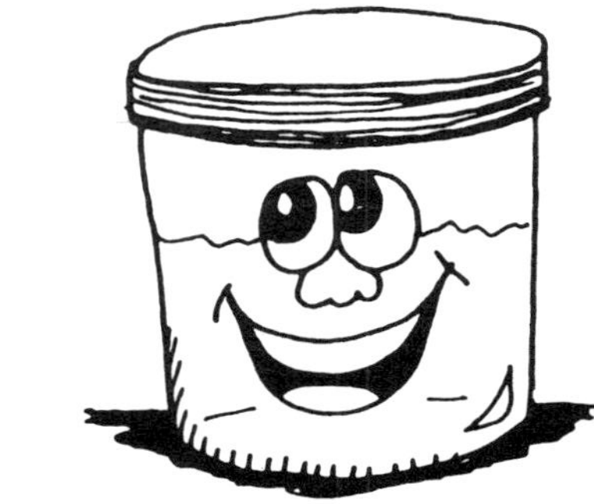

• Draw a series of pictures showing what happens when oil, water, and sand are mixed and then allowed to settle.

PREDICTION:	ACTUAL:	PREDICTION:	ACTUAL:	RESULT:

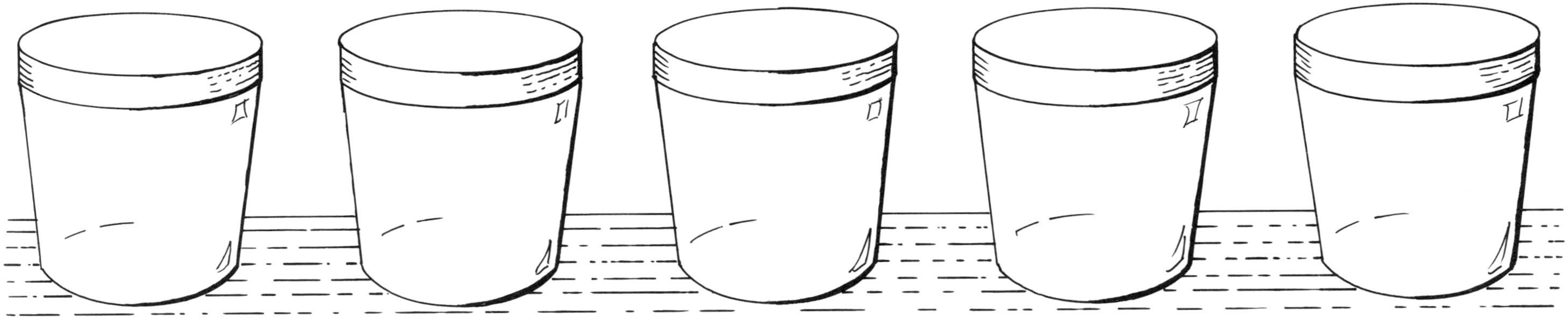

Draw what you think the jar will look like after pouring in the water, oil, and sand.	After Pouring	Draw what you think the jar will look like 10 minutes after it has been shaken.	Immediately After Shaking	After Settling (10 minutes after the jar has been shaken)

_____cm. of water after shaking

_____cm. of water after settling

"HELP SAVE THE BIRDS!"

I. Topic Area
Water treatment — filtration

II. Introductory Statement
This activity will help students understand the process of filtration, an important step in water purification, by allowing them to devise a system to filter dirty water.

III. Math Skills
a. Measuring

Science Processes
a. Observing
b. Measuring
c. Collecting and recording data

IV. Materials
Per class:
2 liters of pre-made muddy water with small bits of leaves, sticks, sand, etc.
Note: *place all of the following on a class "supply table"* or pass out the following to each group:
2–3 plastic or styrofoam cups
1 graduated beaker to measure 240 ml of dirty water
2 sheets of aluminum foil approximately 12"x 24"
2–3 sheets of paper toweling
1 cup of clean, fine sand
240 ml of dirty water
optional: clean gravel, small aquarium rocks, charcoal, cotton, etc.

V. Key Question
How can you make muddy water cleaner so that it is clear enough for birds to bathe in?

VI. Background Information
Filtration is one method for separating a mixture. Many water treatment plants have 3 basic steps in the process of purifying the water: 1) coagulation and settling, 2) filtration, 3) dissection.

In filtration, water is passed through a bed of sand usually about 2½ feet deep on top of a bed of gravel about 1 foot deep. The water is then treated by adding chlorine to kill disease carrying organisms.

VII. Management Suggestions
1. You may organize this lesson as an open-ended, divergent activity or as a teacher directed lesson.
   a. *For an open ended lesson:* allow the students to select their materials from a "supply table" which has all the materials listed in the lesson plan.
   b. *Teacher directed lesson:* have students all make the same filtering device — step by step — from a given set of materials.

Hints for making a filtering device:
   a. Poke holes in a styrofoam cup and place a paper towel in it to keep the sand and gravel from falling through.
   b. Make a funnel out of aluminum foil and line it with a paper towel and fill it with sand and gravel.

VIII. Procedure
1. Set the stage with the students by asking them to imagine the following situation in a local park:
   "Your town has just experienced a severe rainstorm with some minor flooding. The local park is very soggy and filled with mud holes. The birds used to bathe themselves in the clean water areas in the park but now they are filled with muddy water. How can we clean the water for the birds?"
2. Show students the sign that was posted in the park.
3. Show the students a cupful of muddy water, ask them to design a method for cleaning the muddy water.
4. Allow the students to select the materials from a class "supply table" or pass out materials, as listed above, to each group.
5. Pass out the activity sheet, "Help Save the Dirty Birds" to each group. Discuss page.
6. Have each group construct their filtration system.
7. Have the students measure 240 ml of dirty water and pour it through their filtration system.
8. Collect the filtered water in a separate cup and measure the amount reclaimed. Record the amount and complete the activity sheet.

IX. Discussion Question
Have each group share the procedures they used for cleaning the water and the amount of water they reclaimed. Were the amounts the same or different? If so, why?

X. Extended Activities
1. Collect all the clean water samples from each group and put them outside in a shallow pan for the birds to bathe in around the school. Try to locate the "bird bath" near the classroom so you can check on it during the day.
2. Try placing 4–5 drops of food coloring in the muddy water to represent contaminants in the water system. Observe what happens to the cleansed water with the food coloring in it? Does it filter out? Discuss water pollution.
3. Evaporate a small sample of each group's cleansed water to check for other particles, minerals, etc., that may have been left after filtering.

XI. Curriculum Coordinates:
1. Languare Arts: Write a story explaining how you would filter dirty creek water if you were stranded or lost and needed clean water to live.

Attention All Bird Lovers:

The water in the park is very muddy since the last rainstorm. The birds need clean, clear water in which to wash their feathers.

Please Help Us...

We need someone to find a way to make the water as clean and clear as possible.

Help stamp out "Dirty Birds"!

"Help Save the Birds!"

Members of the "Help Save the Birds" committee:

- ______________
- ______________
- ______________
- ______________
- ______________
- ______________

Draw a picture of your group's filtration system.
Label each item in your system.

List your group's procedures:

Amount of water given to clean = __________ ml.

Amount of water your group cleaned = __________ ml.

Difference = Amount of water trapped in your filter __________ ml.

MINI WATER TREATMENT SIMULATION

I. Topic Area
Water treatment

II. Introductory Statement
Students will do an activity that simulates the steps in the water treatment process.

III. Math Skills
a. Measuring

Sciences Processes
a. Observing
b. Applying and generalizing

IV. Materials
Per group:
1 cup water with approximately ½ tsp. dirt. Stir well
2 clear plasic cups (approximately 10 oz.)
1 styrofoam cup (using a sharpened pencil, poke 10 small holes in bottom for filter cup)
1 small piece of paper toweling to use as a filter
1 tsp. powdered alum from drug store (4 oz. approximately $2.00)
½ to ⅔ cup clean sand
¼ cup clean gravel (optional)
2 drops of **simulated** chlorine (Make up a mixture of yellow food coloring in water to simulate adding chlorine for purification)

V. Key Question
How is water from the natural water cycle purified for home use?

VI. Background Information
A water company must go through several steps to insure safe and pure drinking water for their community.

The water that is processed comes from the natural water cycle and has usually been transferred and stored in a reservoir before processing.

The following steps are found in a typical water treatment plant:
Aeration: Water is sprayed into the air to release any trapped gases and to absorb additional oxygen.
Coagulation: To remove dirt suspended in the water, powdered alum is dissolved in the water and it forms tiny, sticky particles called "floc" which attach to the dirt particles. The combined weight of the dirt and the alum particles (floc) become heavy enough to sink to the bottom during *Sedimentation.*
Sedimentation: The heavy particles (floc) settle to the bottom and the clear water above the particles is skimmed from the top and is ready for *Filtration.*
Filtration: The clear water passes through layers of sand, gravel and charcoal to remove small particles.
Chlorination: A small amount of chlorine gas is added to kill any bacteria or microorganisms that may be in the water.

VII. Management Suggestions
1. This activity may be done without adding the alum. However, if you do add the alum it produces much clearer water. Alum may be purchased at any drug store and costs approximately $2.00 for 4 ounces. The alum creates "floc" which may take 10–15 minutes to settle to the bottom.
2. Clean sand may be purchased from any hardware store for approximately $3.50 per 60 lbs. If you use sand or gravel from the playground be sure to rinse it well first to remove any dirt.
3. A piece of paper towel may be used to line the styrofoam cup to prevent the sand from coming through the holes.
4. A series of styrofoam cups may be stacked one on another to make the most efficient styrofoam filtering system. Each cup could contain a separate material to filter the water through.

VIII. Procedure
1. Discuss water purification. In order to have safe and pure drinking water, the local supply must go through several steps in a treatment process.
2. For each group pass out 1 clear, plastic cup with water that has a ½ teaspoon of dirt mixed in it. Water that has come through the natural water cycle might not be as dirty as this sample.
3. Pass out the activity sheets to each student; review the steps in the water treatment process.
4. Pass out the materials to each group. Have the students poke 10–12 small holes in the bottom of the styrofoam cup. This will be used as a filter cup. Have extra cups available for more elaborate filtering systems. Have the students record their observations on the activity sheet.
5. Students should add 1 or 2 drops of **simulated** chlorine bleach to each groups final water sample. **CAUTION: Do not use real bleach or drink the water!**

IX. Discussion Questions
1. Compare each of the groups samples and have each group share their method of purification.
2. Discuss what would have happened if the steps were done in a different order. Try again — varying the process and compare the results.

X. Extended Activities
1. Students can write letters or phone their local water company asking them to send literature or have a representative visit the class to explain local water treatment procedures.
2. Go on a field trip to the local water facility.
3. Invent their own water purification system using other common objects they may have at home.

Optional Lesson:
Water Treatment Plant — see activity sheet.
a. Cut out each square in rows 2, 3 & 4.
b. Arrange them in the proper order of a water treatment plant.
c. Tape all of the squares together in a long strip and pass it through the slits of the top row.
d. The correct order for the squares is: 1. incoming water; 2. aeration; 3. alum; 4. coagulation; 5. sedimentation; 6. filtration; 7. chlorination; 8. storage; 9. to homes.

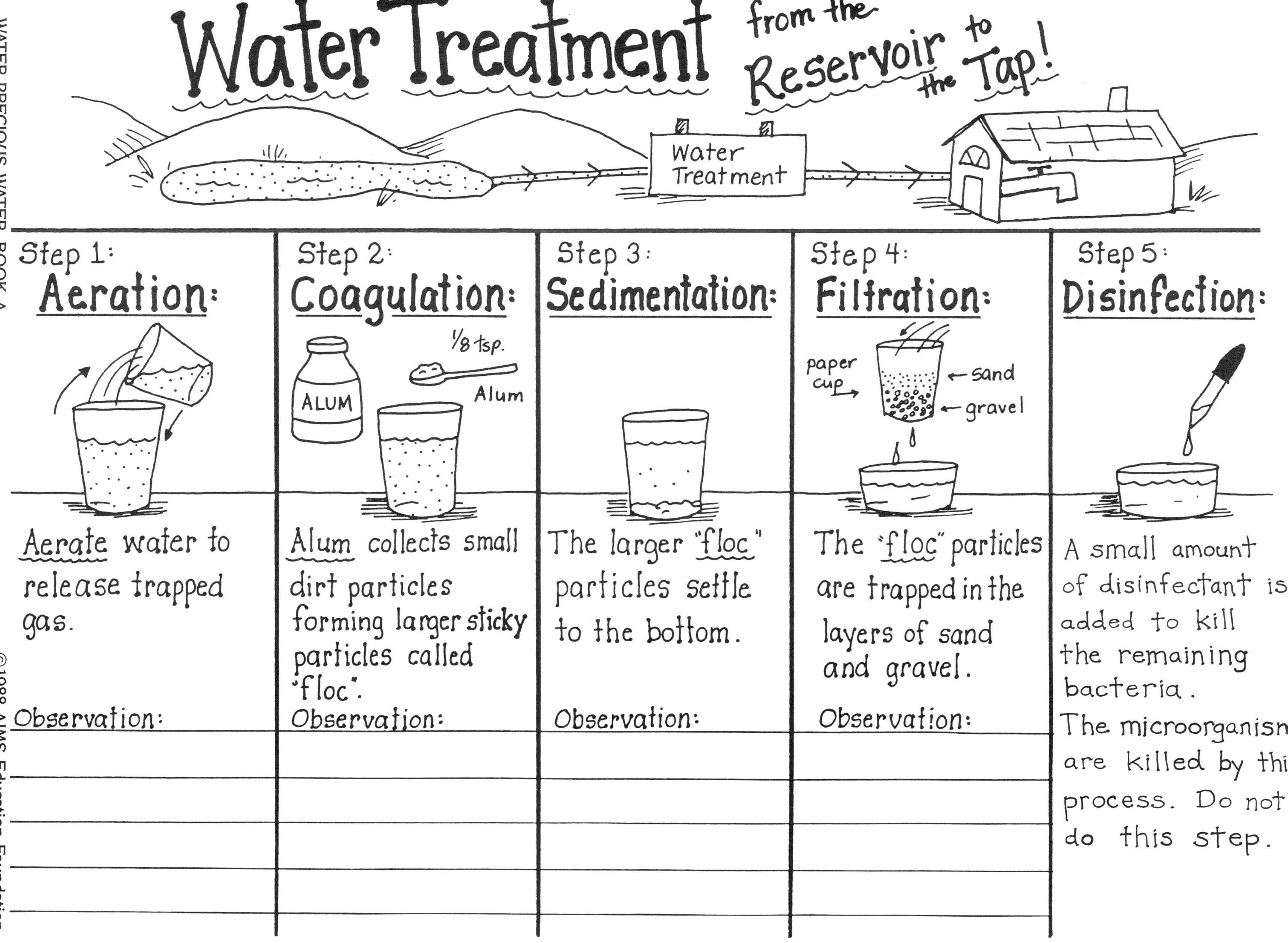
Water Treatment from the Reservoir to the Tap!
Water Treatment
Step 1:
Aeration:
Aerate water to release trapped gas.
Observation:
Step 2:
Coagulation:
ALUM
1/8 tsp.
Alum
Alum collects small dirt particles forming larger sticky particles called "floc".
Observation:
Step 3:
Sedimentation:
The larger "floc" particles settle to the bottom.
Observation:
Step 4:
Filtration:
paper cup
sand
gravel
The "floc" particles are trapped in the layers of sand and gravel.
Observation:
Step 5:
Disinfection:
A small amount of disinfectant is added to kill the remaining bacteria.
The microorganism are killed by this process. Do not do this step.

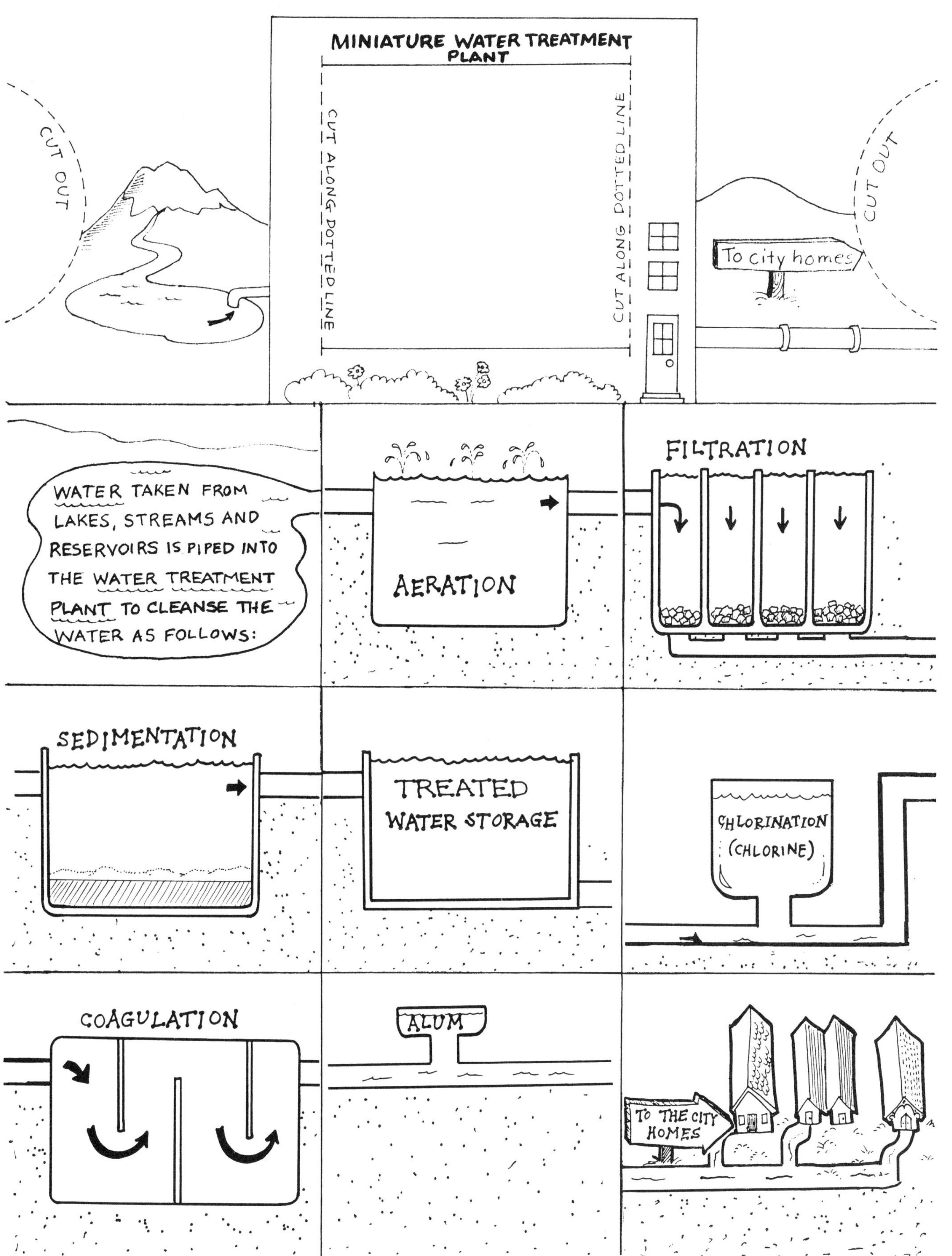
MINIATURE WATER TREATMENT PLANT
CUT OUT
CUT ALONG DOTTED LINE
CUT ALONG DOTTED LINE
CUT OUT
To city homes
WATER TAKEN FROM LAKES, STREAMS AND RESERVOIRS IS PIPED INTO THE WATER TREATMENT PLANT TO CLEANSE THE WATER AS FOLLOWS:
AERATION
FILTRATION
SEDIMENTATION
TREATED WATER STORAGE
CHLORINATION (CHLORINE)
COAGULATION
ALUM
TO THE CITY HOMES

SHAKE, FOAM AND SUDS

I. Topic Area
Hard and soft water

II. Introductory Statement
The students will observe, classify and serial order water samples according to their degree of hardness and softness.

III. Math Skills
a. Serial ordering
b. Measuring

Science Processes
a. Observing
b. Collecting and organizing data
c. Classifying
d. Controlling variables

IV. Materials
Distilled water
Tap water
Bottled water
Salt water
Food coloring
Small cup of soap solution
4 junior baby food jars per group with lids
1 eyedropper per group

V. Key Question
How does the hardness of water affect the amount of suds the water will make?

VI. Background Information
See fact sheet on hard and soft water.

VII. Management Suggestions
1. Mix a salt water solution of 1 tablespoon salt in one liter of tap water.
2. Each group needs 60 ml of each kind of water. (see materials)
3. Use food coloring to color water samples. (red = tap; blue = distilled; yellow = salt; green = bottled).

VIII. Procedure
1. Ask students if all water will make the same amount of suds with equal amounts of soap and amount of shaking.
2. Ask what variables might affect the amount of suds. If hard and soft water is not mentioned, add it to the list.
3. Explain that the softer the water the more suds it will produce (see Fact Sheet).
4. Tell the students they will do an experiment to test different waters for softness.
5. Pass out materials: 4 baby food jars per group, 60 ml of each water sample, 1 eyedropper, liquid soap.
6. Discuss color key on activity sheet. Have students color the jars.
7. Have students color predictions.

Student Directions:
1. Discuss what you think will happen and color in your predictions.
2. Assign one type of water to each group member.
3. Fill each jar with 60 ml of the 4 different water samples.
4. Add 1 drop of liquid soap to each sample and close the lid tightly.
5. Shake all the jars for 1 minute, try to have students use equal force while shaking each jar.
6. Complete the pictures showing the results of your experiment.

IX. Discussion
1. How did your predictions compare to the results?
2. What did you find out about different kinds of water?
3. How will this information be helpful to you?

X. Extensions
1. Make a survey and graph the results to show how many people have soft water in their home.
2. Test other waters like rain or lake water for softness.

XI. Curriculum Coordinates
1. Math: Compare costs of different brands of bottled water and make a graph.
2. Language: Write a letter to a water softener company and ask for more information.
3. Geography: Find and list some places that have naturally soft water.

Name ____________

Question: Does the hardness of water affect the amount of suds the water will make?

Color the key as shown.

Prediction: Using the key, color the jars in order from most suds to least suds.

Actual: Using the key, color the jars from most suds to least suds.

Extension: Using a ruler, measure the height of the foam.

Foam height _____ cm (A) _____ cm (B) _____ cm (C) _____ cm (D)

Which water would you choose to make bubbles? ____________

Why? ____________

HARD WATER - SOFT WATER

Pure water is usually not found anywhere on Earth. Pure water would be only H_2O, Hydrogen and Oxygen atoms. Most water is a mixture of H_2O and many other minerals. As rain water soaks into the soil it picks up minerals and gradually becomes mineral rich. Water that is full of minerals is called hard water. Soft water has little calcium and magnesium in it. Water that is distilled is water that has been softened or water that has few minerals in it.

Hard water causes problems in plumbing pipes because it deposits minerals on the sides of the pipes. These minerals will build up in time and cause deposits.

Pipe with no deposits — Pipe with deposits

Are there any mineral deposits on your showerhead at home? Hard water does not allow much sudsing to occur.

It is "hard" to get it to lather!

Soft water produces more suds and is better for cleaning purposes. Many people have soft water machines in their homes. These machines use salts to remove the calcium and magnesium from their tap water.

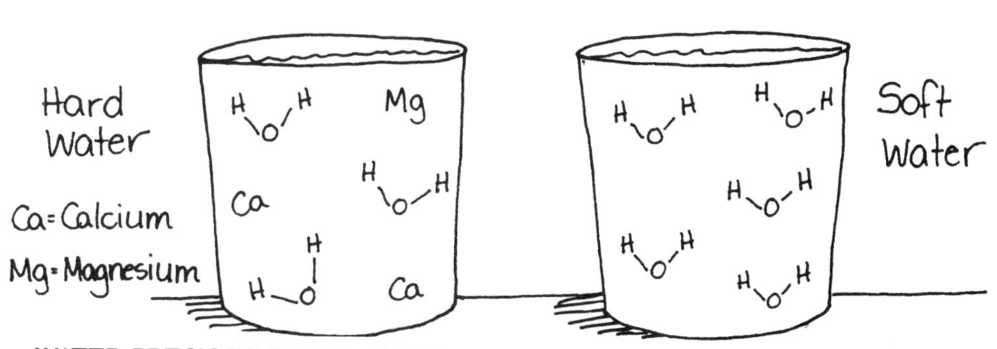

Hardly Soft
How to make Hard Water
1) Fill a cup with 100 ml of Distilled water.
2) Add 1 teaspoon Epsom salt to the distilled water.
Testing your Hard water
1) Add ½ teaspoon of soap to your hard water.
2) Shake for 30 seconds.
3) Measure the height of soap bubbles on top of the water.
4) Draw a picture showing the same number of ml ___.
100 ml.
SOAP
30
How to make Soft Water
1) Fill a cup with 100 ml of Distilled water.
2) Add a pinch of borax to the distilled water.
Testing your Soft water
1) Add ½ teaspoon of soap to your soft water.
2) Shake for 30 seconds.
3) Measure the height of soap bubbles on top of the water.
4) Draw a picture showing the same number of ml ___.
___ml.
___ml.

TASTE TESTERS

I. Topic Area
Water quality

II. Introductory Statement
Students will conduct a "taste test" and analyze subjective data obtained to determine the taste of drinking water.

III. Math Skills
a. Computation
b. Averaging
c. Serial ordering
d. Graphing

Science Processes
a. Hypothesizing
b. Data gathering
c. Controlling variables
d. Drawing conclusions

IV. Materials
1 gallon tap water
1 gallon distilled water
1 gallon bottled water (Brand X)
1 gallon bottled water (Brand Y)
1 - 3 ounce paper cup per student
1 box of unsalted crackers (optional)
activity sheets

V. Key Question
By using our sense of taste, can people tell the difference between various water samples?

VI. Background Information
Many factors affect the taste of water. Some of these factors are: the mineral content (hardness and softness), the amount of dissolved oxygen, pollution, pH levels, level of chlorine, dissolved metals such as iron, lead, etc. and bacterial content. These factors are considered in the process of water purification. Water taken from various sources may be slightly different in its chemical composition. This difference can affect our sense of taste. This lesson is written to test a person's ability to discriminate between different samples of water.

VII. Management Suggestions
1. Select 4 water samples — tap, bottled (Brand X), bottled (Brand Y), and distilled.
2. Divide the class into 6 groups. Give each group approximately 8 ounces of each sample. Label them A,B,C, and D. Be sure the students don't know the names of the samples.
3. Caution students not to mix the samples. Accurate record keeping is critical.
4. If possible, give a new cup for each taste sample. If not, be sure to wipe out the cup with a paper towel after tasting.
5. A small unsalted cracker may be eaten between trials to eliminate the taste of the previous sample.

VIII. Procedure
1. Ask the class if they think they can tell the difference between bottled and tap water.
2. Discuss water quality — a) hard water, b) clarity, c) chlorine, d) aeration (dissolved oxygen), e) taste, etc.
3. Discuss ways water is cleaned a) filtration, b) chlorination.
4. Distribute activity sheet and discuss. Tell the class they are going to be taste testers. They will be sampling four different water samples — tap, bottled (x), bottled (y) and distilled. *DO NOT* tell the students what the samples are.
5. The students will rate the samples on a scale of 1–10 with 10 being the best. Review how critics rate movies using this scale. Students may give 2 samples the same score if necessary.
6. Give each group of 4–5 students a sample (8 ounces) of each kind of water, A,B,C, and D. Label the containers, be sure not to mix them.
7. Have the students write a hypothesis.
8. Allow each student to take a taste (2 ounces) of each water sample and rate it, recording the scores on the data table.
9. Have each group total their scores for each sample.
10. Have a spokesperson from each group read the total scores for each sample. The rest of the class records this shared data on the table. Example: group 1 sample A = 10, 8, 6, 8 = Total for A of 32. Have all six groups report their totals to the class.
11. Find the class totals and average the scores.
12. Complete the data analysis and graph.

IX. Discussion Questions
1. Discuss results and write conclusions.
2. Discuss error analysis. How could we have run the test to be sure we only tested one variable? Consider the order of the samples. Did everyone try (A) first and (D) last? Would this matter?
3. What qualities do people look for in drinking water?
4. How is our water made suitable for drinking?
5. Can people tell the difference between water types?

X. Extended Activities
1. Research the ways distilled water is produced and used.
2. Using the same water, put food coloring in several samples and see if the food coloring affects taste.
3. Make a poster showing the qualities of drinking water.
4. Take water samples from several locations in your community and repeat the "taste test."

Name ____________________

TASTE TESTERS

Question: By using our sense of taste, can people tell the difference between various water samples?

Hypothesis: ____

On a scale of 1 to 10 rate the following water samples (10=most liked, 1=least liked).

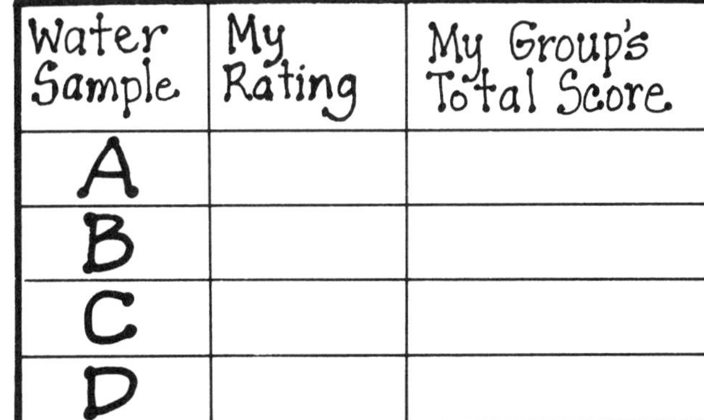

Water Sample	My Rating	My Group's Total Score
A		
B		
C		
D		

Choose me!

Total Scores for Each Group							Class Total Scores	÷	Number of Students in Class	=	Aver. Score
GROUPS→ / SAMPLES↓	#1	#2	#3	#4	#5	#6					
A								÷		=	
B								÷		=	
C								÷		=	
D								÷		=	

Rank the samples by letter from most to least liked.

They loved me!

most ⟷ least

? Was I that bad?

Graph the average score for each of the different water samples.

	A	B	C	D
10				
9				
8				
7				
6				
5				
4				
3				
2				
1				
0				
	A	B	C	D

Now write in our water sample names and see who we are!

The guessing is over.

Conclusions: ______________________________

____

____

____

____

"LITTLE SPROUTS"

I. Topic Area
Water pollution

II. Introductory Statement
In this lesson, students will see the effects of watering seeds with polluted water.

III. Math Skills
a. Comparing

Science Processes
a. Observing
b. Gathering and recording data
c. Applying and generalizing

IV. Materials
Per student:
1 sandwich size baggie
paper towel
4 pre-soaked lima bean seeds
Per class:
4-2 liter soda bottles filled with different watering solutions as follows:
solution 1 – tap water
solution 2 – salt water - 1 cup salt per 2 liter bottle
solution 3 – soap water - ½ cup liquid soap per 2 liter bottle
solution 4 – vinegar - use vinegar right out of the bottle

VI. Background Information
Water is essential for life. Most seeds will begin to germinate when soaked in water. In some sections of the country, the salt content in the soil is very high and may affect the plant life in the area. Soap and detergents may represent pollutants that can contaminate the water and affect plant growth. The vinegar represents acids that could result from acid rain, pesticides and other industrial chemicals. Vinegar is about 5% acetic acid and 95% water.

VII. Management Suggestions
1. Pre-soak approximately 150 large lima beans overnight (lima beans from the grocery store work well for this experiment).
2. Make a large bulletin board garden scene with 4 sections for each of the different solutions.

VIII. Procedure
1. Discuss what a seed needs to sprout.
2. Ask students if they think seeds would grow if they were given water that was polluted with other substances such as salt, soap, or vinegar. Suggest that they try each solution and see what happens.
3. Divide the class into groups of 4 and assign a different solution to each student in the group.
4. Pass out 1 baggie, 1 paper towel and 4 pre-soaked seeds to each student. Label each baggie with the student's name and solution.
5. Fold the paper towel in half and then in half again. Fold up the bottom edge of the quarter section to form a "pouch" to place the seeds on and staple it in place.
6. Poke a small hole through the paper towel "pouch" below each seed. The roots will be able to grow down through the hole to reach the watering solution in the bottom of the baggie.
7. Insert the paper towel and seeds into the baggie and staple it to the baggie. Make sure part of the paper towel hangs down into the water solution so that the paper towel will be kept moist to hasten germination.
8. Pre-mix each watering solution in 2 liter soda bottles for easy access by the students.
9. Have each student pour about 70 ml of their solution into their baggie, moistening the paper towel and the seeds completely.
10. Each baggie may be stapled to a garden scene on the bulletin board or taped to a sunny window.
11. Have the students draw a picture of their seed's growth on their activity sheets.

IX. Discussion Questions
1. Did all the seeds start to grow?
2. Which seeds grew at the beginning of the experiment? at the end?
3. What did the seeds look like when they stopped growing?
4. Why do you think they stopped growing?
5. Which liquid would you choose to water your seeds?

X. Extended Activities
1. Experiment with other types of seeds by following the same procedures.
2. Transplant seeds into larger pots at the end of the last observation.

XI. Curriculum Coordinates:
1. Math: Students can measure how long the roots are each day.
2. Social Studies: Find out if lima beans will grow in your area. When is the best time to plant them (see seed packet for lima bean seeds)?
3. Language: Write a story pretending to be a lima bean in a garden. Tell about the other plants and garden visitors.
4. Cooking: Make lima beans with the class.
5. Recipe: Use 1 package of dried lima bean seeds.
   a. Rinse. Add 2½ times as much water as beans. Soak overnight.
   b. Add salt, cover and simmer in the water used for soaking for 1 hour. You may add a little onion and celery for added taste.

LITTLE SPROUTS

Name ________________

I am watering my seeds with ________________

SOIL SOAKERS

I. Topic Area
Water penetration and porosity of soil

II. Introductory Statement
Students will discover the rate at which water will soak into various soils.

III. Math Skills	**Science Processes**
a. Data gathering	a. Hypothesizing
b. Computation	b. Interpreting data
c. Graphing	c. Drawing conclusions
d. Measuring	
e. Serial ordering	

IV. Materials
Per group:
- metric ruler
- coffee can (3 lb. size with top and bottom cut off)
- 2 liter plastic soft drink containers or buckets with water
- watch with second hand
- measuring cup — 250 ml (8 ounce cup = 240 ml)
- digging tools — metal spoons, screwdrivers, etc.

Note: smaller coffee cans may be used (1 lb. size)

V. Key Question
How does the type of soil and its location affect the rate and depth of water penetration?

VI. Background Information
The rate at which water will soak into soil is determined by the type of the soil and its compaction. Soil that is very porous will readily accept water. Soil that has been compacted will not absorb water easily and much of the water will either run off or evaporate. Hard packed soils composed of clay allow very little water percolation. Soils that are already saturated do not easily absorb more water and the excess water is lost to run off or evaporation.

VII. Management Suggestions
1. Divide the class into groups of 4–5 students.
2. If smaller coffee cans are used, decrease the amount of water added. (100 milliliters)
3. Select soil samples that vary in compaction — i.e. sand, rocky soil, packed clay, soil recently dug up, soil frequently walked on, etc.
4. It is best to do this activity when the soil is fairly dry. However, it is good to test a sample that is already saturated with water.
5. This lesson can be done over a 3 day period. Students can gather data on day 1 and do the graph and conclusions on day 2. Soil Soakers II could be done on day 3.

VIII. Procedure
1. Divide the class into groups and distribute materials to each group: can, container filled with water, watch with second hand, and the activity sheet.
2. Discuss ground water and how the water soaks (percolates) into the soil.
3. Discuss the question to be tested — (see activity sheet).
4. Explain that the coffee can will be pushed and rotated into the ground about 2 centimeters, then students will pour 250 ml of water into the can. If the water leaks around the edges, continue rotating the can until it stops. Students will record the time it takes for the water to be absorbed into the soil sample. They should run 2 trials of each soil location, however they should move the can for each test, as the soil will already be saturated from trial 1. Be sure that the 2 trials are done very close to each other.
5. Tell the students to hypothesize (see activity sheet) what will occur. They should test at least 3 different soil locations, i.e., sand, hard packed soil, wet soil, loose soil, etc. Students should use a digging tool to dig up the soil for the loose soil sample.
6. Go out to the play yard and have students select the areas that they want to test. Record the data on the activity sheet. There are 6 spaces for location types on the activity sheet. You may not have time to do all 6.
7. The students will turn and push the can so that it is 2 centimeters into the soil sample. They pour the 250 ml of water into the can and time how long it takes to soak into the ground. Repeat near the first location for trial 2.
8. Select other areas to test — i.e., sand, wet soil, packed clay, etc.
9. Return to the classroom and average the data, analyze the data and graph it. Students will have to determine the time intervals to be used on the graph. This will depend on the types of soil tested. Have a discussion as to the numeric intervals to be used.
10. Draw conclusions based on the data.

Soil Soakers II
Repeat the activity on another day with "Soil Soakers II". Students will find the depth that water soaks into the soil in at least 3 different locations. They will use a digging tool (spoon or screwdriver) and a ruler to find dry soil and measure the depth of that soil.

IX. Discussion Questions
1. What happened when the can was placed on sand? Why?
2. What would happen if you put the can on clay? Why?
3. How can you change soil that doesn't soak up water well into soil that absorbs water more readily?
4. How does soil get compacted?
5. Why did the loose soil absorb quickly?
6. Why is it important to keep your garden soil well dug up?

X. Extended Activities
1. Bring a sample of each soil tested into the classroom and analyze and classify them.
2. Select soil from one location and compact one-half of it and compare the percolation rate of the compacted sample to the uncompacted one.
3. Plant seeds in soils of various compaction.
4. Do AIMS activity "Disappearing Drips" — from *Our Wonderful World.*

XI. Curriculum Coordinates
1. Language Arts: write a story about a seed who lands on compacted soil.
2. Art: color or paint a landscape in which a part of the area is lush with vegetation and other parts are barren. Discuss.

QUESTION HOW DOES THE TYPE OF SOIL AND ITS LOCATION AFFECT THE RATE AT WHICH IT SOAKS UP WATER?

HYPOTHESIS ______________________________

____

____

DATA GATHERING Do at least 3 different locations

LOCATION	SOIL TYPE	TIME TO ABSORB TRIAL 1	TIME TO ABSORB TRIAL 2	TOTAL OF BOTH TRIALS	AVERAGE ÷ total by 2
1.			+	=	
2.			+	=	
3.			+	=	
4.			+	=	
5.			+	=	
6.			+	=	

DATA ANALYSIS

1. WHICH SOIL LOCATION HAD THE HIGHEST AVERAGE TIME? ____________
2. WHICH SOIL LOCATION HAD THE LOWEST AVERAGE TIME? ____________
3. RANK THE SOIL LOCATIONS FROM THE MOST ABSORBENT TO THE LEAST ABSORBENT.

SOIL SOAKERS

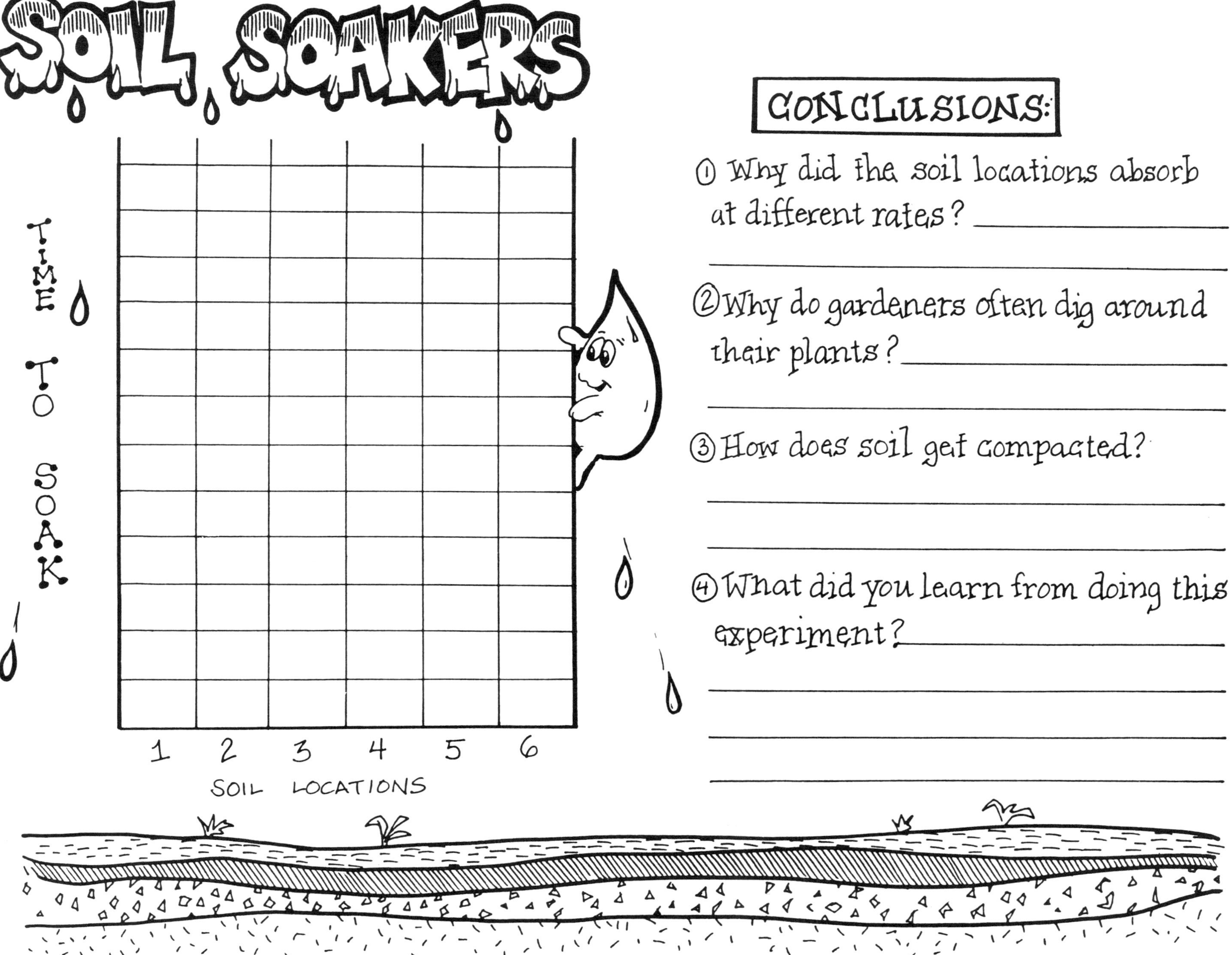

CONCLUSIONS:

1. Why did the soil locations absorb at different rates? ____________
2. Why do gardeners often dig around their plants? ____________
3. How does soil get compacted? ____________
4. What did you learn from doing this experiment? ____________

QUESTION: DOES WATER SOAK INTO DIFFERENT DEPTHS IN DIFFERENT SOIL SAMPLES?

PREDICTION:

SOIL SAMPLE	Depth of water penetration in cm:
1	
2	
3	
4	
5	

RESULTS:

SOIL SAMPLE	Actual depth of water penetration in cm:
1	
2	
3	
4	
5	

Water soaking in

CONCLUSIONS:

① Which sample had the deepest water penetration? Why?

____

② Which sample had the shallowest water penetration? Why?

____

③ How can you increase the depth water will penetrate the soil? ______________________________

RAIN AWAY

I. Topic Area
Erosion

II. Introductory Statement
Students will observe the effects of erosion caused by rain on a bare hillside.

III. Math Skills
a. Measuring
b. Comparing
c. Computation

Science Processes
a. Observing
b. Predicting
c. Collecting data
d. Generalizing

IV. Materials
Per group:
- cookie sheet or large shallow pan
- book — approximately 1–1½" thick covered with plastic wrap or block of wood
- 300 ml mixed dirt and sand
- 10 ounce cup (optional)
- styrofoam cup
- tape
- centimeter ruler
- calibrated cup or beaker
- green, brown & blue crayons

V. Key Question
What happens to soil on a bare hillside when it rains?

VI. Background Information
Erosion is the wearing away of land surface by various natural forces. The most important causes of erosion are wind, water and ice. Erosion can be controlled if slopes are covered with vegetation or terraced.

VII. Management Suggestion
Be sure sand and dirt mixture is moist enough to form into a hill. Divide class into groups of 4–6.

VIII. Procedure
1. Teams form a hill out of sand and dirt at one end of the pan. They can use a cup as a form for the hill or make their own. Elevate the pan so that the hill is at the higher end. Be sure to use an object to elevate it that will not be damaged by water.
2. Draw a picture of the hill in the pan marked "BEFORE" on the activity sheet.
3. Poke three holes in the bottom of the styrofoam cup using only the very sharp point of a pencil. Cover holes with tape.
4. Fill the cup with 200 ml of water.
5. Hold the cup about 12 centimeters above the hill. Pull the tape from under the cup and allow the "rain" to fall.
6. Once all 200 ml has fallen, draw what the pan and hill look like on the activity sheet labeled "After 1st Rain". Show where the dirt is, what the hill looks like and where the water is located.
7. Do not rebuild the hill. Repeat steps four and five. Draw the results on the activity sheet labeled "After the 2nd rain."
8. Feel the dirt at the bottom of the pan and the dirt at the base of the hill. Is there a difference? Why?
9. Pour water from the pan into the beaker. Record the amount of the runoff on the data table.
10. Compute the difference between the original 400 ml of rain water and the total amount of run off.

IX. Discussion Questions
1. What happens to the dirt when rain falls?
2. How could the dirt be kept on the hill during a rain?
3. Why would it be better to keep the dirt on the hill?
4. Where did most of the dirt settle, at the base, midway or all the way down?
5. Why do you think it dropped where it did?
6. What if it had rained harder and therefore, faster? What would have happened to the dirt then?
7. Where do you think the missing water went?

X. Extended Activities
1. Try doing the same experiment with a variety of soil types.

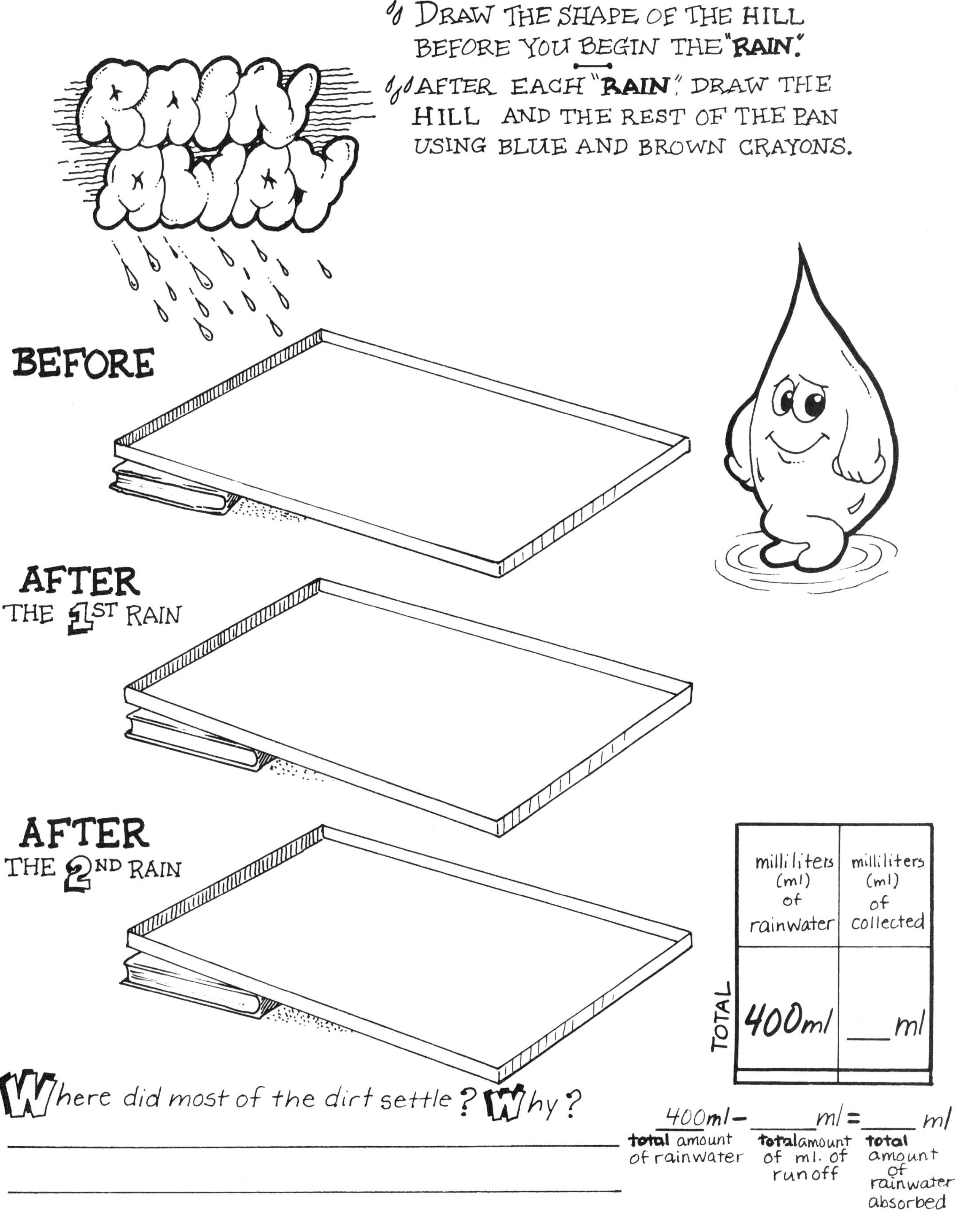

	milliliters (ml) of rainwater	milliliters (ml) of collected
TOTAL	400ml	___ml

400ml – _____ml = _____ ml

total amount of rainwater – **total** amount of ml. of runoff = **total** amount of rainwater absorbed

Where did most of the dirt settle? Why?

____

____

____

DON'T RAIN AWAY

I. Topic Area

Erosion

II. Introductory Statement

Students will observe how vegetation helps control the erosion caused by rain.

III. Math Skill

a. Measuring

Science Processes

a. Observing
b. Predicting
c. Collecting data

IV. Materials

Per group:

- cookie sheet or large shallow pan
- book — approximately 1–1½″ thick covered with plastic wrap or block of wood
- 300 ml mixed dirt and sand
- 10 ounce cup (optional)
- styrofoam cup
- tape
- centimeter ruler
- calibrated cup
- green, brown & blue crayons

V. Key Question

How can water erosion on a hillside be controlled?

VI. Background Information

Erosion is the wearing away of land surface by various natural forces. The most important causes of erosion are wind, water and ice. Erosion can be controlled if slopes are covered with vegetation or terraced.

VII. Management Suggestions

1. Be sure sand and dirt mixture is moist enough to form into a hill.
2. Divide class into groups of 4–6.

VIII. Procedure

1. Allow students to gather grass, leaves, sticks, roots, etc.
2. Students follow the same procedures as in "Rain Away" except in this activity they will cover their hills with the materials collected to simulate slopes covered with vegetation.

IX. Discussion Questions

1. What effect did covering the hill with "vegetation" have when it rained?
2. Compare the results of "Rain Away" and "Don't Rain Away."
3. Why is there more erosion in the hills after a fire?
4. What else can be done to lessen erosion caused by rain?

X. Extended Activities

1. Terrace the "hills" and repeat the activity.
2. Plant rye grass on the "hills" and allow it to grow, then repeat the activity.

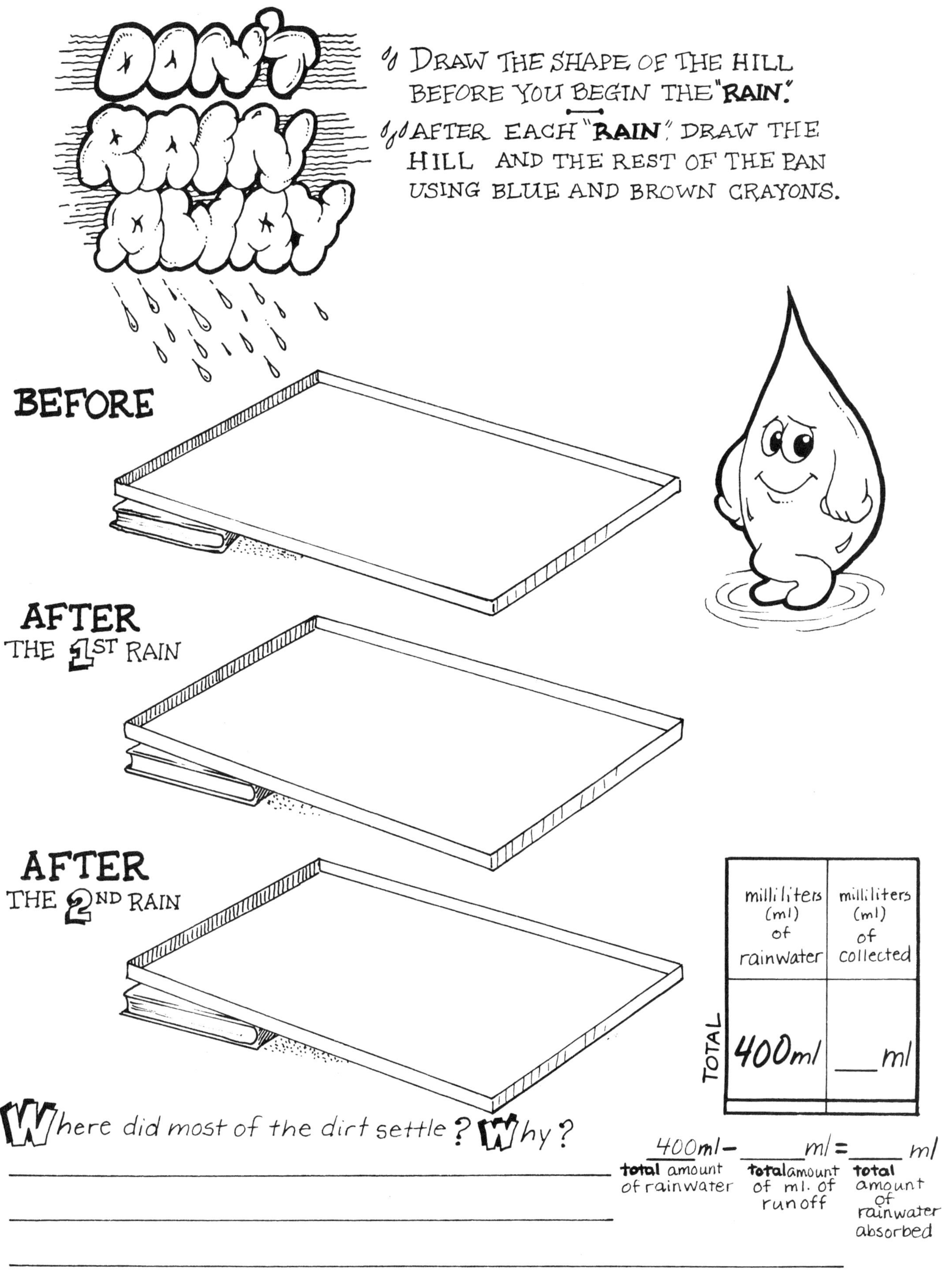

	milliliters (ml) of rainwater	milliliters (ml) of collected
TOTAL	400ml	___ml

Where did most of the dirt settle? Why?

____

____

____

400ml − ____ml = ____ ml

total amount of rainwater − **total** amount of ml. of runoff = **total** amount of rainwater absorbed

WATER ISLAND

I. Topic Area
Water distribution

II. Introductory Statement
This is an open-ended activity designed to emphasize the importance of sharing a limited natural resource, in this case water, throughout a given area. The students are encouraged to use higher level thinking skills to solve the water distribution problem by designing an efficient water system. There are many possible water systems. The real value of this activity comes in the discussion and analysis of possible solutions and the realization that natural resources such as water must be shared by all.

III. Math Skills
a. Computation
b. Comparing
c. Sequencing

Science Processes
a. Observing
b. Collecting data
c. Comparing
d. Drawing conclusions
e. Applying and generalizing

IV. Materials
9 island maps (2 pages)
9 sources and distribution page
9 construction items page
9 group cost comparison sheets
crayons
glue
scissors

V. Key Question
What is the least expensive way to design a water system that would deliver 1,000 gallons of water to each city?

VI. Background Information
There are various sources of water. Water is obtained from ground water sources, fresh water lakes, rivers, man-made lakes, and desalinization plants. The following list defines some of the parts of a water system.
Reservoir — a storage area for water.
Aqueduct — a man-made canal or distribution system.
Pipeline — pipes that carry water on top or underground.
Pump station — a station that is necessary to pump water around a city or over elevated terrain.
Dam — a means of storing water in a reservoir or lake.
Well — a means of obtaining ground water.
Water purification plant — a plant that purifies water.
Ground water — the water table - an underground water supply.
Desalinization — a process of removing salt from ocean water.

VII. Management Suggestions
1. This is a simulation and the rules should be adjusted to meet your classes needs.
2. Divide the class into teams of 2 to 4.
3. Each team will receive one 2 page "Island Map", 1 construction items sheet, 1 construction rules and cost sheet, and 1 group cost comparison sheet.

VIII. Procedure
1. Pass out the island map pages and have students tape them together. Discuss the geographical features with the students. Each student will color the surface water sources blue and color the underground water purple.
2. Ask the students to describe each city and discuss possible ways to supply its water. List these ideas on the board.
3. Discuss the key question and divide the students into teams.
4. Hand out the construction rules and items sheets to each team and as a class discuss the benefits, drawbacks, and uses of each item.
5. Explain that each source or distribution method has both a point value related to cost and a maximum amount of water it can provide.
6. Students will plan one or more solutions to the water needs of both cities. Their goal is to design a system that will bring 1,000 gallons of water to any point along the city limits line using the least amount of points.
7. The student cost analysis sheet lists the rules to be followed. Remind students to observe these rules.
8. The team determines their best solution. They will cut and paste it in place on the island map.
9. Students will write an explanation of their distribution plan. They should total the cost of their systems and record (points).
10. Allow time for each group to share their final plan with the class. Each teams' results should be recorded on the group cost comparison sheet.
11. Have 2 groups meet to share and compare their water maps and distribution plans. Complete item #2 on group sheet.
12. Optional: repeat the above activity using 1 "Fate Card" per group. Adjust the water system accordingly.

IX. Discussion Questions
1. How were the water needs of each city different?
2. Explain the process you used to make your first plan?
3. Did your first plan change? Explain.
4. What did you learn about how geography affects the distribution of water?
5. What is the danger of having a single source of water?
6. How are the water storage and distribution systems in our area different than those on Water Island?

X. Extended Activities
1. Make an efficient water network between the two cities.
2. What type of industry would each city have?
3. Repeat the activity and assign varying populations and water demands to each city. Each person would need 100 gallons of water.
4. Repeat the activity with a polluted lake, rivers and/or ground water.

XI. Curriculum Coordinates
1. Social Studies:
   a. Research an island to find out how the island's water is supplied.
   b. Add coordinates to the island map. Select a location for a hidden treasure and give directions so the students can find the treasure.

BLUE OCEAN
CITY A
RED RIVER
(100 gallons per day)
ground water
5 water drops = water for 1 well

N
W
E
S
CITY B
"CLEAR LAKE"
800 gallons per day
"GREEN RIVER"
(200 GALLONS PER DAY)
"YELLOW RIVER"
(200 GALLONS PER DAY)

Construction Rules

ITEM: SPECIAL NOTES:	COST: POINTS	GALLONS OF H_2O PER DAY
1. 1 Well = 5 raindrops of ground H_2O	20 points	100 gallons
2. 1 Dam with Reservoir (all rivers require dams)	100 points	—
3. 1 Pump Station - needed for each of the following: • water purification plant • well • desalinization plant • every 3 pipelines/aqueducts	30 points	—
4. 1 Water Purification Plant / H_2O Storage (One per city)	60 points	—
5. 1 Desalinization Plant	300 points	400 gallons
6. 1 Section of Aqueduct / Pipeline (pipelines cannot be shared)	10 points	—

WATER·SYSTEM·COST·SHEET

CITY A			CITY B		
ITEM:	COST IN POINTS	TOTAL GALLONS H_2O	ITEM:	COST IN POINTS	TOTAL GALLONS H_2O
1.			1.		
2.			2.		
3.			3.		
4.			4.		
5.			5.		
6.			6.		
7.			7.		
8.			8.		
TOTAL:			TOTAL:		

RESERVIOR DAM 100 | RESERVIOR DAM 100 | RESERVIOR DAM 100 | RESERVIOR DAM 100

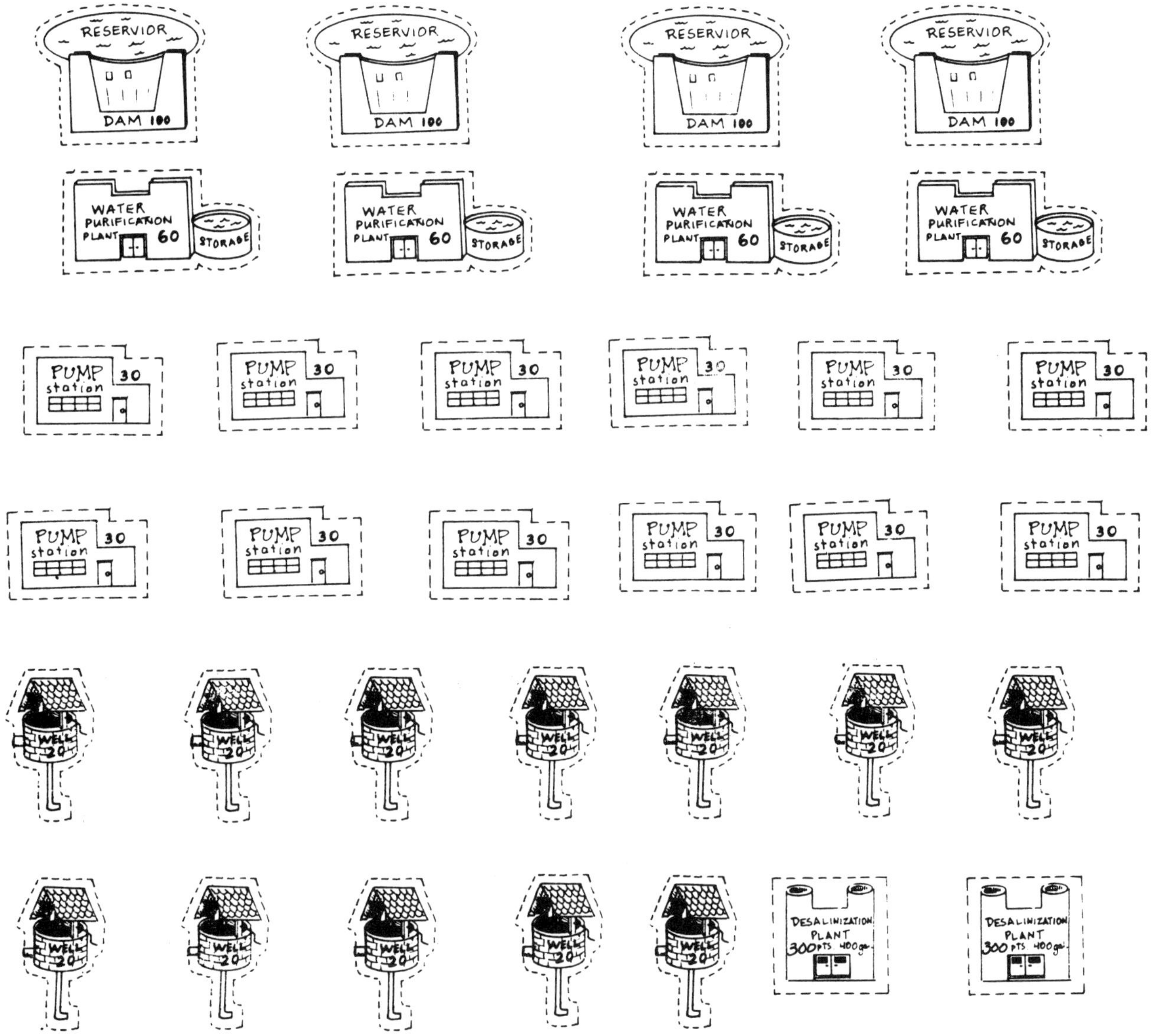

WATER PURIFICATION PLANT 60 STORAGE | WATER PURIFICATION PLANT 60 STORAGE | WATER PURIFICATION PLANT 60 STORAGE | WATER PURIFICATION PLANT 60 STORAGE

PUMP station 30 | PUMP station 30 | PUMP station 30 | PUMP station 30 | PUMP station 30 | PUMP station 30

PUMP station 30 | PUMP station 30 | PUMP station 30 | PUMP station 30 | PUMP station 30 | PUMP station 30

WELL 20 | WELL 20 | WELL 20 | WELL 20 | WELL 20 | WELL 20 | WELL 20

WELL 20 | WELL 20 | WELL 20 | WELL 20 | WELL 20 | DESALINIZATION PLANT 300 PTS 400 ga. | DESALINIZATION PLANT 300 PTS 400 ga.

PIPELINES / AQUEDUCTS

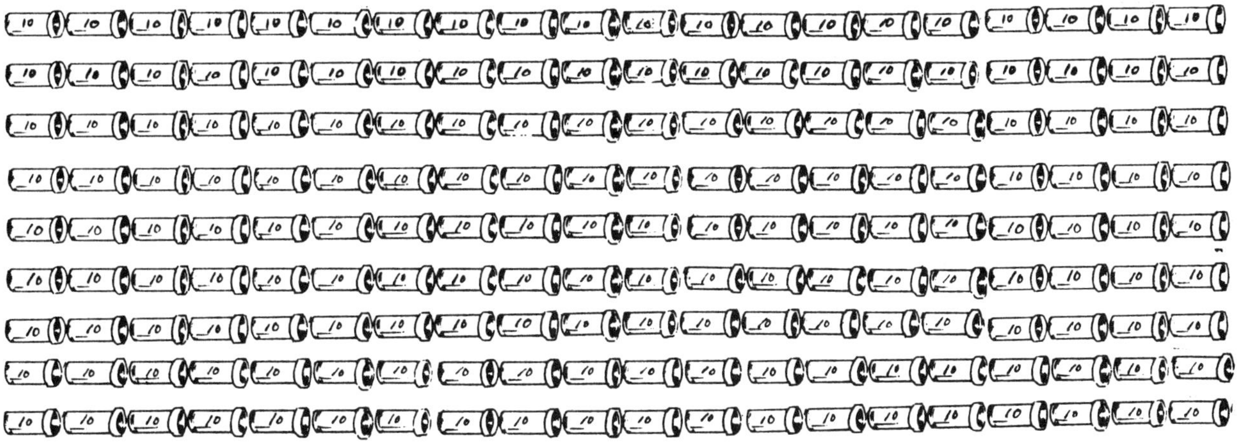

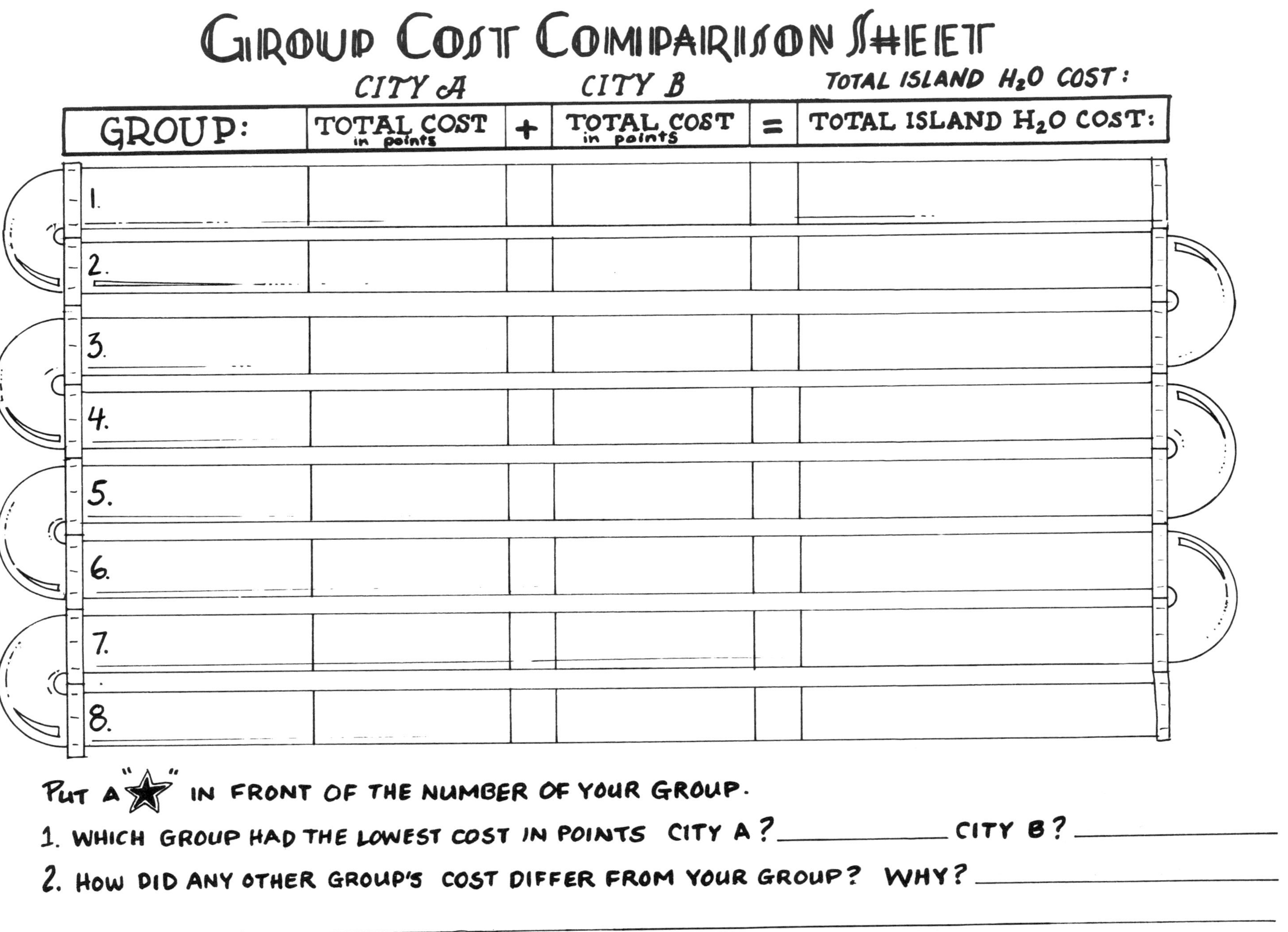

GROUP COST COMPARISON SHEET

GROUP:	CITY A TOTAL COST in points	+	CITY B TOTAL COST in points	=	TOTAL ISLAND H_2O COST: TOTAL ISLAND H_2O COST:
1.					
2.					
3.					
4.					
5.					
6.					
7.					
8.					

PUT A "★" IN FRONT OF THE NUMBER OF YOUR GROUP.

1. WHICH GROUP HAD THE LOWEST COST IN POINTS CITY A? ________ CITY B? ________
2. HOW DID ANY OTHER GROUP'S COST DIFFER FROM YOUR GROUP? WHY? ________

DROUGHT

IN THE SOUTHWESTERN REGION, FOR THE LAST THREE YEARS, LOW RAINFALL HAS REDUCED THE GROUND WATER SUPPLY BY

20 drops.

THE **SALT** CONTENT IN THE WATER HAS **INCREASED!**

THE SALT NEEDS TO BE REMOVED FROM THE WATER AND THE COST FOR **WATER PURIFICATION** IS DOUBLED!

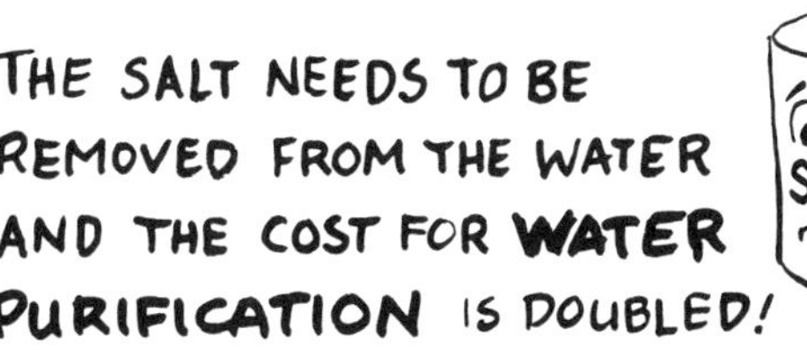

PLEASE ADJUST YOUR COST SHEET or REDESIGN YOUR WATER SYSTEM

DROUGHT

LOW SNOWPACK FOR THE LAST 2 YEARS HAS PRODUCED A REDUCTION IN THE AMOUNT OF WATER IN THE LAKE BY 200 GALLONS.

ADJUST YOUR WATER SYSTEM.

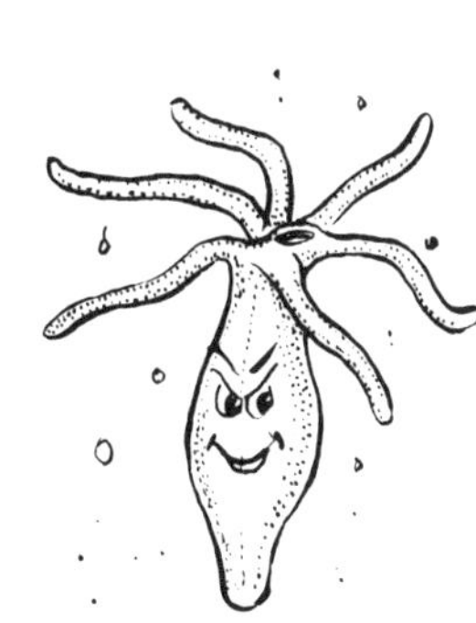

A ***PARASITE*** HAS MULTIPLIED IN THE GREEN RIVER.

NO WATER CAN BE USED FOR 2 YEARS.

ADJUST YOUR WATER SYSTEM

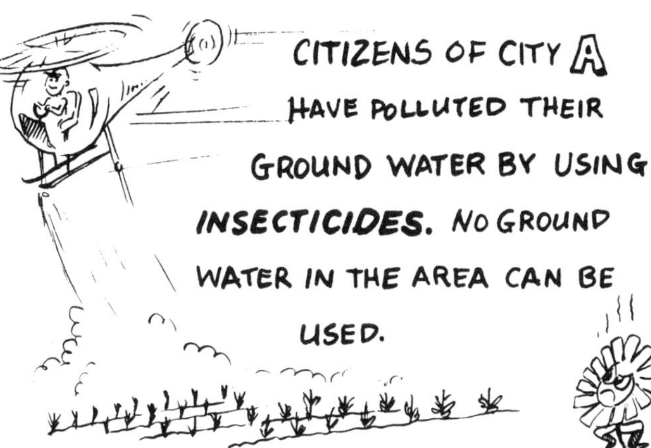

CITIZENS OF CITY A HAVE POLLUTED THEIR GROUND WATER BY USING ***INSECTICIDES.*** NO GROUND WATER IN THE AREA CAN BE USED.

CITY A's POPULATION HAS INCREASED. YOU WILL NEED TO INCREASE THE WATER SUPPLY TO

1500 GALLONS PER DAY.

THE FACTORY HAS DUMPED THEIR SLUDGE INTO THE **YELLOW RIVER.**

NO WATER CAN BE USED!

FLOODING HAS **WASHED OUT** THE **AQUEDUCTS** AND **REROUTED THE GREEN RIVER 5 cm** SOUTH ON YOUR MAP.

REBUILD YOUR AQUEDUCT SYSTEM.

WATER FACTS

I. Topic Area
Water facts

II. Introductory Statement
Students will participate in a cooperative learning lesson in which they will be exposed to a variety of interesting facts about water.

IV. Materials
32 question cards
1 answer sheet per group

VII. Management Suggestions

1. Prepare the question cards ahead of time. They should be cut apart and glued to construction paper or tag board. They can be colored and laminated for future use.
2. Put class in groups of 4 students. Each group needs a passer and a recorder.
3. Discuss the social skills necessary for reaching a group decision. Encourage all group members to participate. Discuss acceptable ways to disagree with someone's answer.
4. Be sure the recorder is aware that each card has a number. The group's answer needs to be written on the correct number line.
5. Set up a system to pass the 4 cards on to the next group. Select a passer from each group to pass the cards.
6. Caution students not to mark on the cards.
7. These cards are designed to stimulate thinking and discussion. The logic used in discussing an answer is perhaps more important than the answer itself.

VIII. Procedure

1. Divide the class into 8 groups, be sure they are heterogeneously mixed.
2. Have each group select a recorder. The recorder will write down the answers to the true/false questions. The recorder should number the answer sheet from 1 to 32.
3. Tell the class that they are going to be given 32 true/false statements. They are to discuss the questions and arrive at a group answer. The recorder will write down that answer. Emphasize that they may not know the correct answer for each question, but that they are to share ideas and come up with a group answer.
4. Each group will begin with 4 question cards. The group will have a few minutes to finish each set of 4 cards. The teacher should let each group know when time is up, and they will pass their set of cards to the next group. Keep the same rotation each time. The groups will pass the cards 8 times, until each group has had all 32 questions.
5. Refer to the key and read the answers and the explanatory statements. Discuss the answers with the students. Accept answers that have a logical base even if it differs from the key. See * on key.

IX. Discussion Questions

1. Which of the cards had answers that were surprising to you?
2. What are some ways we can conserve water?
3. Tell a partner 4 things you learned from the activity. Reverse the roles and repeat.

X. Extended Activities

1. Choose a card and make a water conservation poster.
2. Do some research on water and make up 4 fact cards of your own.
3. Devise activities that demonstrate some of the facts learned.

WATER FACTS

Answer Key

1. True* — at sea level water boils at 100 °C (212 °F), but the boiling point of water decreases as air pressure decreases. High in the mountains water will boil at a lower temperature.
2. True — steam is invisible. The cloud seen is condensed water. Steam would be the invisible portion of the air between the tea kettle and the cloud.
3. False — books list the percentage anywhere from 60% to 90%.
4. True — H_20 – However it is very rare to find a single water molecule.
5. False — 15–30 gallons are used. A low flow shower head uses about 3 gallons a minute. A standard head uses about 8 gallons a minute.
6. True
7. True
8. False — 97% is in the salty oceans.
9. True
10. False — about 40% is used.
11. True
12. True
13. False — about 70 gallons per day.
14. True
15. False — 32 °F or O °C.
16. True* — it contracts for 0 °C – 4 °C, then expands.
17. False* — pure water is not a good conductor. When a person is wet the person loses his resistance and becomes a good conductor.
18. False — it expands – it is rare for a substance to expand when frozen.
19. False — due to surface tension, many insects can.
20. True
21. False — due to surface tension, a free falling drop is round.
22. True* — if you leave the hose running.
23. True
24. False — water is denser than oil, and an equal volume is heavier.
25. False — it takes about 100,000 gallons to manufacture a car.
26. True — hydrogen and oxygen – H_20.
27. True — in capillary action in plants, water molecules are attracted to one another and are pulled up to the top of the plant.
28. True
29. False — much of the water will evaporate and the water will not reach the plant's roots.
30. True — this is why you add salt to water when boiling pasta.
31. True
32. True* — however this depends on the temperature of the environment.

*Accept answers, true or false, if the answer is based on some logical explanation.

WATER FACT CARDS

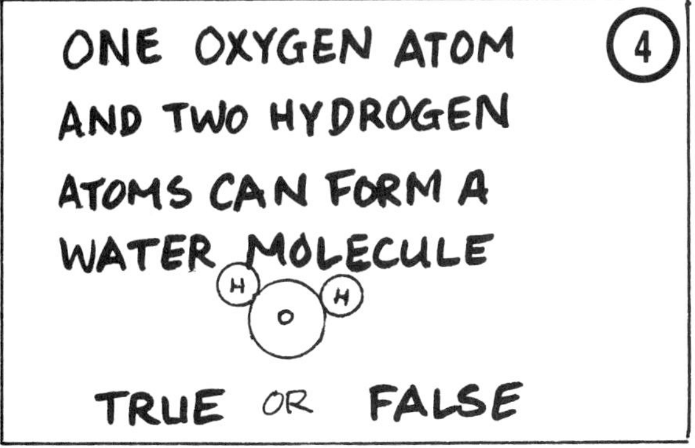

9
Cola
IT TAKES 10 GALLONS OF WATER TO PRODUCE 1 can of COLA
TRUE OR FALSE

10
THE TOILET TANK USES 30% of your home's water.
TRUE OR FALSE

11
WATER IS THE MOST COMMON SUBSTANCE ON EARTH.
TRUE OR FALSE

12
It takes 115 gallons of water to grow enough wheat to make a loaf of BREAD.
TRUE OR FALSE

13
Every AMERICAN uses 30 gallons of water a day in their home.
TRUE OR FALSE

14
SNOW
is a form of PRECIPITATION
TRUE OR FALSE

15
BR-R-R!!
WATER WILL FREEZE AT 32° C.
TRUE OR FALSE

16
Water will expand when heated.
TRUE OR FALSE

17
WATER IS A GOOD CONDUCTOR OF ELECTRICITY.
TRUE OR FALSE

21
WHILE FALLING, A DROP OF WATER IS SHAPED LIKE A TEARDROP.
AHHHH
TRUE OR FALSE

18
WATER CONTRACTS WHEN FROZEN.
TRUE OR FALSE

22
WASHING A CAR USES ABOUT 100 GALLONS OF WATER.
TRUE OR FALSE

19
ANIMALS CANNOT WALK ON LIQUID WATER.
TRUE OR FALSE

23
THE PREFIX "HYDRO" means "WATER".
TRUE or FALSE

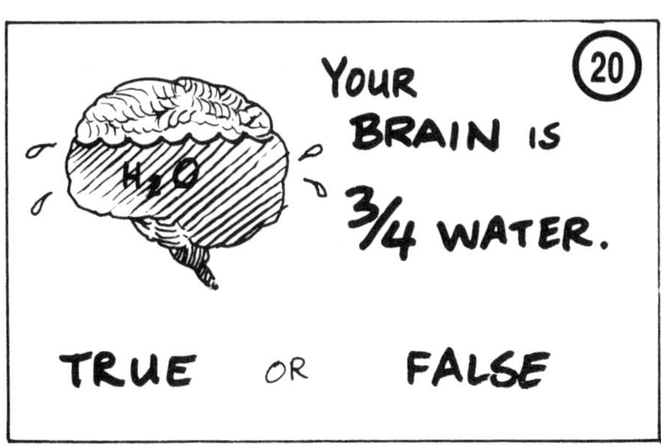
20
YOUR BRAIN IS 3/4 WATER.
H2O
TRUE OR FALSE

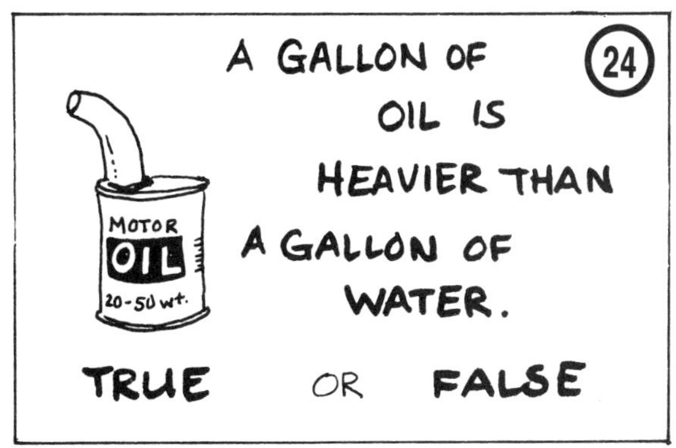
24
A GALLON OF OIL IS HEAVIER THAN A GALLON OF WATER.
MOTOR
OIL
20-50 wt.
TRUE OR FALSE

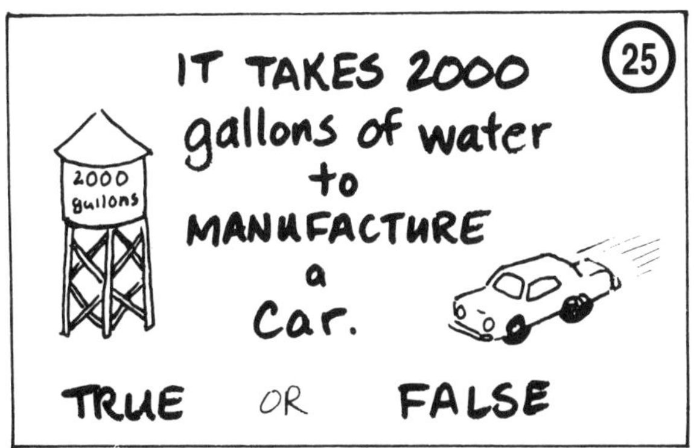
25
IT TAKES 2000
gallons of water
to
MANUFACTURE
a
Car.
2000 gallons
TRUE OR FALSE

IT IS BEST TO
WATER THE LAWN
WHEN IT
IS HOT
AND WINDY
29
TRUE OR FALSE

26
WATER
IS MADE UP OF TWO
COLORLESS AND ODORLESS
gases.
hydrogen + oxygen =
TRUE
OR
FALSE

Adding Salt to water
will cause it to
BOIL at a higher
TEMPERATURE.
30
SALT
TRUE OR FALSE

WATER CAN
FLOW
UPHILL.
27
TRUE
OR
FALSE
"Celery"

DEW IS A FORM
OF
CONDENSATION
31
TRUE OR FALSE

28
THE
AMOUNT OF
WATER VAPOR
IN THE AIR
IS CALLED
HUMIDITY.
TRUE OR FALSE

A PERSON COULD
LIVE WITHOUT WATER
FOR ABOUT A
WEEK.
32
TRUE OR FALSE

WATER OLYMPICS

I. Topic Area
Properties of water

II. Introductory Statement
This is a series of four activities that deal with some of the properties of water. The activities are short and may be done one at a time or all together in an "olympic" format. The activities can be used as an introduction to a water unit with the students discovering some of the properties of water, or they can be used as culminating activities. Either way, it is important that the children discuss the properties of water they have observed after doing the activities.

III. Math Skills
a. Computation
b. Measuring

Science Processes
a. Observing
b. Predicting
c. Collecting and recording data
d. Controlling variables

IV. Materials
Amazing Water Race:
roll of wax paper, copies of water maze, tape, eyedropper, toothpicks, liquid soap
Fold and Float:
aluminum foil cut in five inch squares, bowls for water
Paper Towel Absorption:
three different brands of paper towels, rulers, bowls or cups for water
Bubble Rings:
liquid soap, straws, centimeter rulers, cups

V. Key Question
See task cards for each activity.

VI. Background Information
Amazing Water Race: Water molecules are attracted to each other because of their molecular structure. This attraction of like molecules is called cohesion. This causes water molecules to want to stay together unless the cohesive bonds are weakened. Soap weakens the strong bonds between water molecules.
Fold and Float: Aluminum should sink when placed in water because it has a density which is greater than that of water. However, when a piece of aluminum foil is placed flat on the surface of water, it will often float. This is because the surface tension of water is strong enough to hold up the aluminum foil even though it is 2.7 times denser than water. Surface tension is caused by the cohesion between water molecules. The molecules below the surface of the water are attracted equally in all directions, while those on the surface are only attracted to the sides and downward. This causes the surface of the water to contract and act like it is covered with a thin film. The surface tension of water is strong enough to hold up some objects that are more dense than water. This is why some insects, like the water strider, are able to walk on the surface of water.
Paper Towel Absorption: Water is able to travel through the narrow spaces between the fibers of paper towels by capillary action. The attractive force between the water molecules and the paper fibers is greater than the cohesive force between the water molecules. This causes the water molecules to be pulled up the paper towel against the force of gravity. The attraction between unlike molecules is called adhesion.
Bubble Rings: See the background information in the "Bubble Busters" activity in this book.

VII. Management Suggestions
These four activities may be done as individual lessons or as centers in an "olympic" format with students rotating through the activities. The task cards can be run off and placed at each center. Students should be responsible for cleaning up a center before moving on to the next one. An extra supply of paper towels may be placed at each center to facilitate clean up. It is important that these activities be followed by class discussions which focus on the water properties involved.

VIII. Procedure
The procedures for each activity are given on the task cards but some students may need each activity demonstrated before starting. The task cards may be run off and placed at each center. If the students are doing the activities as part of a water olympics, they will each need a copy of the score card. The students must make a prediction and record it on the score card before doing each event. The person with the lowest score is the winner.

The following are special instructions for the four events.
Amazing Water Race: Tape a piece of wax paper over each maze before starting. After doing the two activities for this event you may want to have students observe the effect of soap on the cohesion of water by dipping a toothpick into liquid soap and then touching a large water drop with it. Make sure that you have fresh water, toothpicks and wax paper if you repeat this activity or the soap left on the maze or toothpick will spoil the results for the next group.
Fold and Float: This activity could be extended with older students to cover fractions. Each time you fold the foil in half you are decreasing its area by a power of two. After three folds you have only one eighth of the original surface area, after four folds you have only one sixteenth.
Paper Towel Absorption: The paper towels can be cut beforehand into strips. The school's paper towel can be used as one of the three brands tested for absorption rate. The students can tape the three strips to a pencil so they can dip them simultaneously into the bowl of water.
Bubble Rings: Mix the bubble solution beforehand by adding 30 ml (2 tablespoons) of liquid soap to the water in a two liter plastic bottle. Place 4–6 cups of bubble solution on the table along with a box of straws. The students will each get their own straw when blowing bubbles and then will use centimeter rulers to measure the diameter of the ring that is left on the table when the bubble bursts.

IX. Discussion Question
The discussion should center on the properties of water that the students observed at each center. See the background information for a description of the water properties for each activity.

WATER OLYMPICS

	EVENT:	PREDICTION:	ACTUAL:	DIFFERENCE:
1	A-MAZING H_2O RACE	________ sec.	________ sec.	________
	H_2O STRETCH	________ cm	________ cm	________
2	FOLD 'N FLOAT	________ folds	________ folds	________
3	PAPER TOWEL ABSORPTION ($\frac{0 \text{ if correct}}{5 \text{ pts. if wrong}}$)	PAPER TOWEL #____	PAPER TOWEL #____	RIGHT 0 OR WRONG 5
4	BUBBLE RINGS	________ cm	________ cm	________
			TOTAL DIFFERENCES	________

* REMEMBER to subtract the lower number from the higher number.

* Keep your difference as low as possible.

AMAZING WATER RACE

Make water droplet this size

START

FINISH

TAPE A PIECE OF WAX PAPER ON TOP OF THE MAZE.

Fold 'n Float

• Question: How many times can you fold a 5"x5" piece of aluminum foil until it sinks? How small can you go?

• Things you need: 1 bowl (2/3's full of H_2O), 1 5"x5" piece of aluminum foil

1. Float the 5"x5" foil in the water.
2. Predict the number of folds that cause the foil to sink.
3. Fold it in half – (that's your 1st fold) – place it in the water. Does it float?

4. If so... fold it in half again – (that's your 2nd fold) – does it float?
5. Keep folding the foil in half and testing whether or not it floats after each fold.
6. Keep making the "surface area" of the foil smaller until it sinks.

A-Mazing

Event: · H_2O · Race ·

Question: How can your water drop be guided through the maze?

Procedure:

① Tape a piece of wax paper on top of the maze.

② Place a water drop to fit inside the circle on your paper.

③ Move the water drop through the maze with a toothpick. If the drop separates, go back and collect it before you continue.

④ Time how long it takes to move the drop through the maze.

Question #2: **Predict** – how far can you stretch the drop of water * Find the difference between the prediction and the actual length.

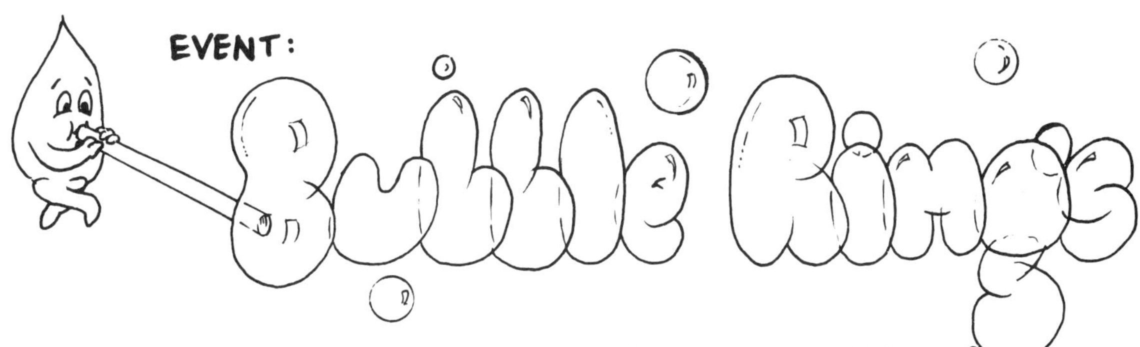

Question: *How large a bubble can you blow?*

You need: 1 straw per person, bubble solution, 1 cm. ruler

Procedure:
1. Wet table top or paper plate surface.
2. Trap bubble solution into straw.
3. Place straw angled on the table top and blow gently.
4. Measure diameter of bubble after it pops.

PAPER TOWEL EVENT: ABSORPTION
PAPER TOWEL RACE

- 0 POINTS IF YOUR PREDICTION IS CORRECT
- 5 POINTS IF YOUR PREDICTION IS WRONG. ☺

QUESTION: WHICH BRAND OF PAPER TOWELS ABSORBS THE WATER THE FASTEST?

MATERIALS: 1 STRIP - 1" x 8" - OF EACH BRAND OF PAPER TOWEL PER GROUP
1 BOWL OF WATER

PROCEDURE: PREDICT WHICH BRAND IS THE FASTEST TO ABSORB H_2O.

- MARK EACH STRIP AT THE 18 cm MARK.
- PLACE 1 STRIP FROM EACH OF THE TEST STRIPS INTO A BOWL OF H_2O ALL AT THE SAME TIME.
- THE WATER REACHES THE 18 cm MARK ON WHICH STRIP FIRST?
- COMPARE THE PREDICTION WITH THE ACTUAL RESULTS. IF YOUR PREDICTION WAS THE FASTEST THE DIFFERENCE IS 0; IF NOT, GIVE YOURSELF 5 POINTS IN THE DIFFERENCE COLUMN.

The AIMS Program

AIMS is the acronym for "**A**ctivities **I**ntegrating **M**athematics and **S**cience." Such integration enriches learning and makes it meaningful and holistic. AIMS began as a project of Fresno Pacific University to integrate the study of mathematics and science in grades K-9, but has since expanded to include language arts, social studies, and other disciplines.

AIMS is a continuing program of the non-profit AIMS Education Foundation. It had its inception in a National Science Foundation funded program whose purpose was to explore the effectiveness of integrating mathematics and science. The project directors in cooperation with 80 elementary classroom teachers devoted two years to a thorough field-testing of the results and implications of integration.

The approach met with such positive results that the decision was made to launch a program to create instructional materials incorporating this concept. Despite the fact that thoughtful educators have long recommended an integrative approach, very little appropriate material was available in 1981 when the project began. A series of writing projects have ensued and today the AIMS Education Foundation is committed to continue the creation of new integrated activities on a permanent basis.

The AIMS program is funded through the sale of this developing series of books and proceeds from the Foundation's endowment. All net income from program and products flows into a trust fund administered by the AIMS Education Foundation. Use of these funds is restricted to support of research, development, and publication of new materials. Writers donate all their rights to the Foundation to support its on-going program. No royalties are paid to the writers.

The rationale for integration lies in the fact that science, mathematics, language arts, social studies, etc., are integrally interwoven in the real world from which it follows that they should be similarly treated in the classroom where we are preparing students to live in that world. Teachers who use the AIMS program give enthusiastic endorsement to the effectiveness of this approach.

Science encompasses the art of questioning, investigating, hypothesizing, discovering, and communicating. Mathematics is a language that provides clarity, objectivity, and understanding. The language arts provide us powerful tools of communication. Many of the major contemporary societal issues stem from advancements in science and must be studied in the context of the social sciences. Therefore, it is timely that all of us take seriously a more holistic mode of educating our students. This goal motivates all who are associated with the AIMS Program. We invite you to join us in this effort.

Meaningful integration of knowledge is a major recommendation coming from the nation's professional science and mathematics associations. The American Association for the Advancement of Science in *Science for All Americans* strongly recommends the integration of mathematics, science, and technology. The National Council of Teachers of Mathematics places strong emphasis on applications of mathematics such as are found in science investigations. AIMS is fully aligned with these recommendations.

Extensive field testing of AIMS investigations confirms these beneficial results.

1. Mathematics becomes more meaningful, hence more useful, when it is applied to situations that interest students.
2. The extent to which science is studied and understood is increased, with a significant economy of time, when mathematics and science are integrated.
3. There is improved quality of learning and retention, supporting the thesis that learning which is meaningful and relevant is more effective.
4. Motivation and involvement are increased dramatically as students investigate real-world situations and participate actively in the process.

We invite you to become part of this classroom teacher movement by using an integrated approach to learning and sharing any suggestions you may have. The AIMS Program welcomes you!

AIMS Education Foundation Programs

A Day with AIMS

Intensive one-day workshops are offered to introduce educators to the philosophy and rationale of AIMS. Participants will discuss the methodology of AIMS and the strategies by which AIMS principles may be incorporated into curriculum. Each participant will take part in a variety of hands-on AIMS investigations to gain an understanding of such aspects as the scientific/mathematical content, classroom management, and connections with other curricular areas. *A Day with AIMS* workshops may be offered anywhere in the United States. Necessary supplies and take-home materials are usually included in the enrollment fee.

A Week with AIMS

Throughout the nation, AIMS offers many one-week workshops each year, usually in the summer. Each workshop lasts five days and includes at least 30 hours of AIMS hands-on instruction. Participants are grouped according to the grade level(s) in which they are interested. Instructors are members of the AIMS Instructional Leadership Network. Supplies for the activities and a generous supply of take-home materials are included in the enrollment fee. Sites are selected on the basis of applications submitted by educational organizations. If chosen to host a workshop, the host agency agrees to provide specified facilities and cooperate in the promotion of the workshop. The AIMS Education Foundation supplies workshop materials as well as the travel, housing, and meals for instructors.

AIMS One-Week Perspectives Workshops

Each summer, Fresno Pacific University offers AIMS one-week workshops on its campus in Fresno, California. AIMS Program Directors and highly qualified members of the AIMS National Leadership Network serve as instructors.

The Science Festival and the Festival of Mathematics

Each summer, Fresno Pacific University offers a Science Festival and a Festival of Mathematics. These festivals have gained national recognition as inspiring and challenging experiences, giving unique opportunities to experience hands-on mathematics and science in topical and grade-level groups. Guest faculty includes some of the nation's most highly regarded mathematics and science educators. Supplies and take-home materials are included in the enrollment fee.

The AIMS Instructional Leadership Program

This is an AIMS staff-development program seeking to prepare facilitators for leadership roles in science/math education in their home districts or regions. Upon successful completion of the program, trained facilitators may become members of the AIMS Instructional Leadership Network, qualified to conduct AIMS workshops, teach AIMS in-service courses for college credit, and serve as AIMS consultants. Intensive training is provided in mathematics, science, process and thinking skills, workshop management, and other relevant topics.

College Credit and Grants

Those who participate in workshops may often qualify for college credit. If the workshop takes place on the campus of Fresno Pacific University, that institution may grant appropriate credit. If the workshop takes place off-campus, arrangements can sometimes be made for credit to be granted by another institution. In addition, the applicant's home school district is often willing to grant in-service or professional-development credit. Many educators who participate in AIMS workshops are recipients of various types of educational grants, either local or national. Nationally known foundations and funding agencies have long recognized the value of AIMS mathematics and science workshops to educators. The AIMS Education Foundation encourages educators interested in attending or hosting workshops to explore the possibilities suggested above. Although the Foundation strongly supports such interest, it reminds applicants that they have the primary responsibility for fulfilling *current* requirements.

For current information regarding the programs described above, please complete the following:

Information Request

Please send current information on the items checked:

___ *Basic Information Packet* on AIMS materials
___ *Festival of Mathematics*
___ *Science Festival*
___ *AIMS Instructional Leadership Program*
___ *AIMS One-Week Perspectives* workshops
___ *A Week with AIMS* workshops
___ Hosting information for *A Day with AIMS* workshops
___ Hosting information for *A Week with AIMS* workshops

Name ______________________ Phone ______________________

Address ____

Street City State Zip

We invite you to subscribe to *AIMS*!

Each issue of *AIMS* contains a variety of material useful to educators at all grade levels. Feature articles of lasting value deal with topics such as mathematical or science concepts, curriculum, assessment, the teaching of process skills, and historical background. Several of the latest AIMS math/science investigations are always included, along with their reproducible activity sheets. As needs direct and space allows, various issues contain news of current developments, such as workshop schedules, activities of the AIMS Instructional Leadership Network, and announcements of upcoming publications.

AIMS is published monthly, August through May. Subscriptions are on an annual basis only. A subscription entered at any time will begin with the next issue, but will also include the previous issues of that volume. Readers have preferred this arrangement because articles and activities within an annual volume are often interrelated.

Please note that an *AIMS* subscription automatically includes duplication rights for one school site for all issues included in the subscription. Many schools build cost-effective library resources with their subscriptions.

YES! I am interested in subscribing to *AIMS*.

Name ______________________________ Home Phone ____________________

Address ____________________________ City, State, Zip ________________

Please send the following volumes (subject to availability):

	Volume	Years	Price		Volume	Years	Price
_____	Volume V	(1990-91)	$30.00	_____	Volume X	(1995-96)	$30.00
_____	Volume VI	(1991-92)	$30.00	_____	Volume XI	(1996-97)	$30.00
_____	Volume VII	(1992-93)	$30.00	_____	Volume XII	(1997-98)	$30.00
_____	Volume VIII	(1993-94)	$30.00	_____	Volume XIII	(1998-99)	$30.00
_____	Volume IX	(1994-95)	$30.00	_____	Volume XIV	(1999-00)	$30.00

_____ **Limited offer: Volumes XIV & XV (1999-2001) $55.00**
(Note: Prices may change without notice)

Check your method of payment:

❒ Check enclosed in the amount of $ __________

❒ Purchase order attached (Please include the P.O.#, the authorizing signature, and position of the authorizing person.)

❒ Credit Card ❒ Visa ❒ MasterCard Amount $ ______________

Card # ______________________________ Expiration Date ___________

Signature ___________________________ Today's Date ____________

Make checks payable to **AIMS Education Foundation**.
Mail to *AIMS* Magazine, P.O. Box 8120, Fresno, CA 93747-8120.
Phone (559) 255-4094 or (888) 733-2467 FAX (559) 255-6396
AIMS Homepage: http://www.AIMSedu.org/

AIMS Program Publications

GRADES K-4 SERIES

Bats Incredible!
Brinca de Alegria Hacia la Primavera con las Matemáticas y Ciencias
Cáete de Gusto Hacia el Otoño con la Matemáticas y Ciencias
Cycles of Knowing and Growing
Fall Into Math and Science
Field Detectives
Glide Into Winter With Math and Science
Hardhatting in a Geo-World (Revised Edition, 1996)
Jaw Breakers and Heart Thumpers (Revised Edition, 1995)
Los Cincos Sentidos
Overhead and Underfoot (Revised Edition, 1994)
Patine al Invierno con Matemáticas y Ciencias
Popping With Power (Revised Edition, 1996)
Primariamente Física (Revised Edition, 1994)
Primarily Earth
Primariamente Plantas
Primarily Physics (Revised Edition, 1994)
Primarily Plants
Sense-able Science
Spring Into Math and Science
Under Construction

GRADES K-6 SERIES

Budding Botanist
Critters
El Botanista Principiante
Exploring Environments
Mostly Magnets
Ositos Nada Más
Primarily Bears
Principalmente Imanes
Water Precious Water

GRADES 5-9 SERIES

Actions with Fractions
Brick Layers
Conexiones Eléctricas
Down to Earth
Electrical Connections
Finding Your Bearings (Revised Edition, 1996)
Floaters and Sinkers (Revised Edition, 1995)
From Head to Toe
Fun With Foods
Gravity Rules!
Historical Connections in Mathematics, Volume I
Historical Connections in Mathematics, Volume II
Historical Connections in Mathematics, Volume III
Just for the Fun of It!
Machine Shop
Magnificent Microworld Adventures
Math + Science, A Solution
Off the Wall Science: A Poster Series Revisited
Our Wonderful World
Out of This World (Revised Edition, 1994)
Pieces and Patterns, A Patchwork in Math and Science
Piezas y Diseños, un Mosaic de Matemáticas y Ciencias
Proportional Reasoning
Soap Films and Bubbles
Spatial Visualization
The Sky's the Limit (Revised Edition, 1994)
The Amazing Circle, Volume 1
Through the Eyes of the Explorers:
  Minds-on Math & Mapping
What's Next, Volume 1
What's Next, Volume 2
What's Next, Volume 3

For further information write to:

AIMS Education Foundation • P.O. Box 8120 • Fresno, California 93747-8120
www.AIMSedu.org/ • Fax 559•255•6396

AIMS Duplication Rights Program

AIMS has received many requests from school districts for the purchase of unlimited duplication rights to AIMS materials. In response, the AIMS Education Foundation has formulated the program outlined below. There is a built-in flexibility which, we trust, will provide for those who use AIMS materials extensively to purchase such rights for either individual activities or entire books.

It is the goal of the AIMS Education Foundation to make its materials and programs available at reasonable cost. All income from the sale of publications and duplication rights is used to support AIMS programs; hence, strict adherence to regulations governing duplication is essential. Duplication of AIMS materials beyond limits set by copyright laws and those specified below is strictly forbidden.

Limited Duplication Rights

Any purchaser of an AIMS book may make up to *200 copies* of any activity in that book for use at *one school site*. Beyond that, rights must be purchased according to the appropriate category.

Unlimited Duplication Rights for Single Activities

An individual or school may purchase the right to make an unlimited number of copies of a single activity. The royalty is $5.00 per activity per school site.

Examples: 3 activities x 1 site x $5.00 = $15.00
9 activities x 3 sites x $5.00 = $135.00

Unlimited Duplication Rights for Entire Books

A school or district may purchase the right to make an unlimited number of copies of a single, *specified* book. The royalty is $20.00 per book per school site. This is in addition to the cost of the book.

Examples: 5 books x 1 site x $20.00 = $100.00
12 books x 10 sites x $20.00 = $2400.00

Magazine/Newsletter Duplication Rights

Those who purchase *AIMS* (magazine)/*Newsletter* are hereby granted permission to make up to 200 copies of any portion of it, provided these copies will be used for educational purposes.

Workshop Instructors' Duplication Rights

Workshop instructors may distribute to registered workshop participants a maximum of 100 copies of any article and/or 100 copies of no more than eight activities, provided these six conditions are met:

1. Since all AIMS activities are based upon the *AIMS Model of Mathematics* and the *AIMS Model of Learning*, leaders must include in their presentations an explanation of these two models.
2. Workshop instructors must relate the AIMS activities presented to these basic explanations of the AIMS philosophy of education.
3. The copyright notice must appear on all materials distributed.
4. Instructors must provide information enabling participants to order books and magazines from the Foundation.
5. Instructors must inform participants of their limited duplication rights as outlined below.
6. Only student pages may be duplicated.

Written permission must be obtained for duplication beyond the limits listed above. Additional royalty payments may be required.

Workshop Participants' Rights

Those enrolled in workshops in which AIMS student activity sheets are distributed may duplicate a maximum of 35 copies or enough to use the lessons one time with one class, whichever is less. Beyond that, rights must be purchased according to the appropriate category.

Application for Duplication Rights

The purchasing agency or individual must clearly specify the following:

1. Name, address, and telephone number
2. Titles of the books for Unlimited Duplication Rights contracts
3. Titles of activities for Unlimited Duplication Rights contracts
4. Names and addresses of school sites for which duplication rights are being purchased.

NOTE: Books to be duplicated must be purchased separately and are not included in the contract for Unlimited Duplication Rights.

The requested duplication rights are automatically authorized when proper payment is received, although a *Certificate of Duplication Rights* will be issued when the application is processed.

Address all correspondence to: **Contract Division**
AIMS Education Foundation
P.O. Box 8120
Fresno, CA 93747-8120

www.AIMSedu.org/
Fax 559•255•6396